teach yourself®

**magic**

teach
yourself®

**magic**
anthony galvin

For over 60 years, more than
50 million people have learnt over
750 subjects the **teach yourself**
way, with impressive results.

be where you want to be
with **teach yourself**

For UK order enquiries: please contact Bookpoint Ltd, 130 Milton Park, Abingdon, Oxon, OX14 4SB. Telephone: +44 (0) 1235 827720. Fax: +44 (0) 1235 400454. Lines are open 09.00–17.00, Monday to Saturday, with a 24-hour message answering service. Details about our titles and how to order are available at www.teachyourself.co.uk

For USA order enquiries: please contact McGraw-Hill Customer Services, PO Box 545, Blacklick, OH 43004-0545, USA. Telephone: 1-800-722-4726. Fax: 1-614-755-5645.

For Canada order enquiries: please contact McGraw-Hill Ryerson Ltd, 300 Water St, Whitby, Ontario, L1N 9B6, Canada. Telephone: 905 430 5000. Fax: 905 430 5020.

Long renowned as the authoritative source for self-guided learning – with more than 50 million copies sold worldwide – the **teach yourself** series includes over 500 titles in the fields of languages, crafts, hobbies, business, computing and education.

*British Library Cataloguing in Publication Data*: a catalogue record for this title is available from the British Library.

*Library of Congress Catalog Card Number*: on file.

First published in UK 2005 by Hodder Education, 338 Euston Road, London, NW1 3BH.

First published in US 2005 by The McGraw-Hill Companies, Inc.

This edition published 2005.

The **teach yourself** name is a registered trade mark of Hodder Headline.

Copyright © 2005 Anthony Galvin

Typeset by Transet Limited, Coventry, England.
Printed in Great Britain for Hodder Education, a division of Hodder Headline, 338 Euston Road, London, NW1 3BH, by Cox & Wyman Ltd, Reading, Berkshire.

The publisher has used its best endeavours to ensure that the URLs for external websites referred to in this book are correct and active at the time of going to press. However, the publisher and the author have no responsibility for the websites and can make no guarantee that a site will remain live or that the content will remain relevant, decent or appropriate.

Hodder Headline's policy is to use papers that are natural, renewable and recyclable products and made from wood grown in sustainable forests. The logging and manufacturing processes are expected to conform to the environmental regulations of the country of origin.

Impression number    10 9 8 7 6 5 4 3 2
Year                          2010 2009 2008 2007 2006

# contents

**foreword**

Magic is one of the oldest arts, and a form of entertainment that has always had a universal appeal to all ages. Devotees are usually attracted by a box of tricks received at a young age, or coming across a book just like this one, which could open the door to a fascinating hobby, an all-consuming passion, or for some a life as a professional magician.

Whilst at first you may wish to challenge your friends with some simple tricks, the real secret of success is to practise each one until you can perform it with confidence. The way you present the tricks as an entertainment is the all-important secret of success and this is emphasised by the author throughout this book. Choose those which suit your individual style and personality, and rehearse them well and you will be set to amuse your friends and family.

In time you may wish to delve further into magic and most large towns have a club where those of a similar interest meet and exchange ideas, present shows and learn more about the art. The Magic Circle is the most famous of these societies and was formed 100 years ago. Today it has some 1,500 members in 40 countries of the world, with Headquarters in London, housing a library of some 8,000 books, a splendid museum and a fully equipped theatre in which to present modern magic to the public.

Magic as a profession has taken me around the world for 45 years, an exciting life of being paid for doing what would otherwise have been my hobby. Countless enthusiasts of all callings and professions find their lives enriched by being able to amuse their friends and clients, and raise a smile wherever they go. I hope this book may serve as your introduction to the fascinating world of magic.

Alan Shaxon
President of The Magic Circle

epigraph

'This is a must-have book for people of all ages who wish to explore the art of magic.'

Marc Oberon, European close-up magic champion 2005, and international black-art illusionist.

'Within the pages of this book you will find professional calibre mysteries worthy of performance by magicians of any level. Anthony Galvin has broken a few rules and boundaries with this book – absolutely brilliant. Highly Recommended.'

Keith Barry, star of *Close Encounters with Keith Barry* and MTVs *Brainwashed*.

xi

**dedication**

This book is dedicated to my wife Cathy and my children Sam and Katelyn, without whom my natural instincts would kick in, and I would be the laziest man in the world. I also dedicate this to the many friends I have made through magic, and to the performers, past and present, who inspired me through their showmanship, skill, teaching ability, or friendship. These include Paul Daniels, Barry Sinclaire, Penn and Teller, Harry Blackstone Junior, Doug Henning, Derren Brown, Jeff McBride, Marc Oberon, Keith Barry, Geoffrey Durham, Ben Elton, Bill Hicks, and a host of others.

Imagine you are out with your mates for a drink. It's your round and you take out a bundle of blank sheets from your wallet. With a wave of your hand you turn them into bank notes and hand them to the speechless bartender.

Perhaps you are trying to impress a date. You stare deep into his eyes and tell him which starlet he fantasises about – and you are right. Of course he will tell you that you are far sexier than she is.

Maybe you are on a flight and a child three rows down begins screaming. You walk down the aisle, do a few simple tricks and turn that scream into a smile.

Magic has come down from the stages of Vegas and Broadway, and into the streets. More and more people realise that magic is something they can do, and do quite easily. As a hobby it is not expensive, it is very varied, and it can keep you entertained for a lifetime. It can also pay for itself, and may even become a second income, if that is what you want.

I performed my first trick at age seven. My friend Pierce and myself spent an afternoon chiselling a hole in a coffee table. I then cut a hole in a tablecloth. The following day was my seventh birthday, and Pierce hid under the table. I draped the tablecloth over it, and waited for my friends to arrive.

When they were all gathered I took my father's trilby and put it on the table. Pierce pushed a teddy bear rabbit through the hole into the hat, and I had performed the classic Rabbit from a Hat trick – a good place to start.

Everyone was impressed, including my parents. Then my mother saw the hole in the tablecloth and my father saw the hole in the table, and my conjuring career was put on hold for another few years.

By 16 I was performing occasionally at Youth Club events, and at 18 I did my first professional gig, a birthday party show. It went well, but I went to college and didn't pursue it.

Years later I bumped into a magician, and the interest was rekindled. Around the same time my fiancé saw me doing comedy and told me I simply wasn't funny. I needed a gimmick. I went back to the magic.

After a few years I quit my job with a newspaper and devoted myself full-time to entertainment. I do children's shows, touring shows with characters such as Bob the Builder, and adult cabaret work. For colleges and drunken pub audiences I do a hypnosis show, and I will do corporate close-up work if asked. My fiancé became my wife, then became a magician one Christmas when I was double booked, and I had to train her in a hurry.

Now we earn a good living. We spend each Christmas performing at a Santa village in Lapland, and we have toured exotic locations such as the Middle East. We have flexible hours, we meet interesting people, and our income depends on how hard we decide to work. I believe things turned out quite well.

I have friends who also love magic. Some do it as a pure hobby, entertaining their friends. Others do a few parties on the side, particularly when they want to save up for a holiday or a new car. Others make their living at it. The beauty of magic is that there is room for all levels of participation.

A number of years ago a TV special called *Breaking the Code – Magic's Greatest Secrets Revealed* got people talking about magic by showing how a number of famous effects are done. Then New Yorker David Blaine pioneered a new approach to television magic – intimate street magic. Now everyone wants to be a magician. Magic is the new rock and roll, and everyone can get involved.

That is what this book is about. I know anyone can learn magic. My wife learnt in a few weeks, because she needed to. Two friends needed a cash injection. I trained both of them, and they became good performers in remarkably quick time. Neither needs the money anymore, but they both continue to perform because they have grown to love magic.

I know you can learn to become a competent magician, and quicker than you imagine. In this book you will learn a number of tricks with ordinary objects, which will hone your skills. You will learn to handle a pack of cards properly to produce miracles. Tricks with coins, elastic bands, bits of paper, biros, and eggs will follow. There is no need to learn them all. In fact you would be better off picking and choosing. Those tricks that you decide to make your own, practise them until they are perfect. Learn a good entertaining routine, with the right gags. Make it good and it will entertain your spectators. Their feedback will give you the encouragement to take it further.

This book begins with simple effects, and then introduces the basic skills of sleight of hand. After this you will be introduced to various branches of the magical arts – cabaret magic, mentalism, and entertaining children.

Finally, for the ambitious, there is a brief section explaining how you can build your own big illusions.

Interspaced between the chapters are snippets of useful (or useless) information on planning an act, developing your showmanship, and marketing yourself. There is some repetition in these sections, but that is deliberate. Some messages are so important they need to be hammered home repeatedly, like the following two.

---

1 Practise until you have a trick perfect.
2 Don't just practise the trick; practise the presentation.

---

A short practice session regularly is more useful than a long session at irregular intervals.

But above all, enjoy your magic. Perform your tricks every chance you get, and savour the look of bewilderment and joy on the faces of those you entertain.

We are almost ready to begin. All you need are a deck of cards, some elastic bands, some coins of varying dimensions, envelopes, a handkerchief, bits of paper, a biro or pencil, a couple of glass tumblers, and maybe an egg or two. A magic wand is optional, but a smile is essential. Enjoy the show; after all, you'll be the star.

---

**Disclaimer**
The author and publisher take no responsibility for accident, injury or any other consequence of following the tricks herein. Students practise at their own risk.

**01**

**something to
get you started**

In this chapter you will learn:
- Simple tricks you can do right now
- How to stretch a finger or thumb
- How to read minds
- How to make a coin vanish.

A good magician does whatever tricks are just right for his or her audience. Of course there is specialisation – some go in for complex card moves that combine the dexterity of a concert pianist with the speed of a sprinter; others go for stunning large-scale illusions, or mind-bending mentalism. But we all have to start somewhere, and the simple tricks in this chapter are as good a place as any.

But don't be fooled by that simplicity. What makes any one of these tricks work is not how you do it, but how you put it across. All the great magicians know that the magic is in the presentation. That is the beauty of self-working tricks. You can learn the trick in minutes, so you can concentrate all your efforts on selling the effect.

A word of advice before you do any of the following tricks – practise until you know them backwards. Then practise some more. When you perform, do it with confidence. Even if terror is eating at your soul, don't let your audience know.

Remember the five golden rules of magic – practise, practise, practise, practise, and never tell the secrets.

# Five golden rules for practising magic

## Rule 1 – Practise

By now that should be sinking in. Before you went to school you could not write. Now you can write easily. How did you arrive at that happy state? Through practise. That is how you learn to walk without thinking about each step, to drive a car or play a piano. It is the same with magic. Practise makes it second nature.

## Rule 2 – Follow the instructions carefully

I have tried to make the instructions as clear and logical as possible. First is a description of the trick (which rarely does it justice). This is followed by a list of what you need, and how you prepare for the trick. Finally, the instructions are broken down point by point. Read the instructions through, then read them through again with the props in your hands. Then it will all begin to make sense.

At an early point in the production of this book we decided to deliberately limit the number of illustrations used. They say that a picture is worth a thousand words. What they fail to mention is that a picture is often an excuse not to read the thousand words. Read the text with the props in hand, and you will be able to do everything here.

## Rule 3 – Never reveal the secrets

People will constantly ask you how you do the tricks. Some will put all sorts of pressure on you, telling you that they have a fascination with magic and would love to know. Say no. Tell them to go out and buy the book. I always find that if someone really wants to do magic it will be obvious and I will give them any help I can. But if all they want is the secret, they can push off – though you can express this in more diplomatic terms.

## Rule 4 – Practise regularly

You did not learn to read by practising every first Tuesday when it rained. You practised daily. Regularity is important. But don't overdo it. A few minutes every day is far more valuable than an hour once a week, and will keep you interested and enthusiastic.

## Rule 5 – The patter is part of the trick

The patter is what you say when you are performing. When you practise the trick, do it as you will perform it. Do it out loud. If you like use a video camera and watch the results. Don't bother with mirrors. They give a distorted view of what is going on. When a magician says he knows how to do a trick, he means that he knows the secret moves, and he knows the presentation. Don't leave out this important bit.

So much for the rules. We will begin with a few tricks that can be done with nothing. All you need is a pair of hands and a working mind. These will be followed by effects using simple, everyday objects. Some of the effects will involve advance preparation, while others can be done impromptu.

Don't worry if none of these early effects seem to be earth-shatteringly brilliant. They are good enough to fool your audience, and prepare you for the miracles to come. If you go climbing in the Himalayas, you will train in the Mendips. And the Mendips have their own charms.

# A note on gender and handedness

The aim of this book is to simplify magic. For that reason the cumbersome he/she has been dropped in favour of he, or in some cases she. This in no way implies that magic should be a male activity. Since the early days women have risen to the top in the art. In recent years Juliana Chan won the world manipulation title, and there are several brilliant women performing and creating magic. I am married to one of them.

I have also written the instructions from the perspective of a right-handed performer. Again this does not imply that lefties should be left out. If you are left handed, just substitute right for left and left for right as you read the instructions, and everything will fall into place.

# Stretch a finger

Magicians are said to be masters of sleight of hand. This is a slight trick using nothing but the hands, so I hope it counts. The beauty of this is that we carry our hands with us everywhere, so we are always ready to perform.

> Effect: You stretch your thumb until it is nine inches long. You then repeat this with a finger.
>
> Required: Your hands.
>
> Preparation: None.
>
> Degree of difficulty: ✳

## Performance

1 Display your left hand and wiggle all the fingers. Explain that as a magician you have to keep your fingers nimble. Hold your left hand in front of your body, thumb pointing up.

2 Grab your left thumb with your right fist. But as you do this, stick your right thumb out between your right index finger and middle finger. The knuckles of your right hand are facing your spectator.

   If you do this right it will appear as if you have just grabbed your left thumb and the tip protrudes from between your fingers.

3 Pretend to pull on your left thumb, slowly pulling your right hand up so that it appears as if your thumb is stretching. All

you are doing is sliding your right fist up your left thumb.

This looks most effective and deceptive if you grunt a little and look as if you are really putting an effort into stretching your thumb.

4 As you pull, you can bend and twist your thumb, but don't get carried away, or you might give the game away.
5 When nothing but the tip of your left thumb remains inside your right fist, stop pulling, then 'push' your left thumb back to its normal position, removing your right fist.

After stretching your thumb, you are ready to follow it up by stretching your finger. Again, this is not an anatomical anomaly so much as an optical illusion.

6 Hold your left hand out, palm down and fingers outstretched. Put your right hand in the 'gun' position, with the index finger out and the rest closed lightly.
7 Put your right hand under your left hand, with your right index finger pushed between your left index and middle finger.
8 Hold your hands down low – stomach level is fine. Now pull some faces and grunt a bit, then slowly cause your right index finger to grow. What you really do is push it forward. The left hand hides the fact that the whole right hand is moving.
9 Retract your finger by sliding your right hand back again. Now shake out both hands, and announce that your fingers are loosened out enough.

These two effects are illusions. Don't linger too long doing them, or someone will spot the secret. But they are good impromptu stunts.

You can follow these with some more sleight of hand, this time involving what magicians call the paddle move. This is when a small move is masked by a larger move, so that the small move goes unnoticed.

## Losing a finger

Effect: You show that one of your fingers is missing. Instantly you restore it.

Required: A hand.

Preparation: Before you begin, hold your right hand with your palm down. You are looking at the back of your hand. Hold the fingers together, and bend the middle finger down at the joint. On a very cursory examination it could look as if you are missing the tip of your middle finger. This is position one.

Now hold your right hand palm up, and separate your fingers, so that the index and middle fingers are together, and the ring and little fingers are together, but there is a gap between both sets of fingers. Stretch your fingers to make the gap as wide as possible. This is position two. You have got to be able to get your hand into both positions quickly and smoothly. It only takes a few minutes practise.

Degree of difficulty: **∗∗**

## Performance

1 Announce that you have a finger that has been giving you problems. Display your right hand palm down, fingers together. With your left hand reach over the grip the tip of your middle finger, tugging sharply.

2 Immediately put your right hand into position one as you pull your left hand clear.

3 Immediately flip your hand over into position two.

4 Straight away flip back into position one.

5 Continue to flip your hand over from position one to position two a number of times in quick succession. This optical illusion creates the perfect impression that one of your fingers is missing.

6 Bring your left hand back over your right hand, shake out your right hand, and reveal that the middle finger is back to normal.

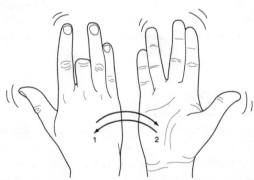

**Figure 1** Losing a finger
Switch hands rapidly from position 1 to position 2 as you turn your palm over.

# Matchstick trick

This is as easy as it gets, so perhaps it's a good one to include this early.

> **Effect:** You place a matchstick in a handkerchief, then snap it in two. When you unfold the handkerchief the matchstick is back in one piece.
>
> **Required:** A white linen handkerchief and two matches.
>
> **Preparation:** Use a man's linen hanky, the sort with a hem. They are less common than they once were, but you can still get them. Tease a hole in the stitching of the hem near one of the corners. Insert a matchstick in this hole and push it into the hem, so that the match is completely concealed. The audience never know it is there.
>
> **Degree of difficulty:** ✳

1 When you are ready to perform, take out the hanky and put it down on the table. Take out a match and put it in the centre of the hanky.
2 Fold up the hanky and grasp the match through the folds. This is what the audience think you are doing. In fact you grasp the match sewn into the hem, and make sure not to touch the other one.
3 Break the match in the hem. The spectators will clearly hear the snap of the match breaking. If you like you can break it a second time.
4 Place the hanky down on the table again, then make some mysterious passes with your hands.
5 Unfold the hanky and the match is back in one piece.

That is how easy magic can be. A four-year-old could do it, and yet it will startle your audience. Next we are going to try something a bit more clever.


# Minds in sympathy

To illustrate how the same effect can be done in different ways, I will explain two different ways of doing this trick. One way is certain, but has faults. The other way eliminates the faults, but the outcome is less certain. All will become clear as you read on.

Effect: Ask a friend to take a key out of his pocket and pass it from hand to hand behind his back. You instantly tell him which hand holds the key. Impressive? He asks you to do it again, and you get it right again. Genuinely puzzled now, he asks for one more chance to catch you out. With a smug smile you tell him that a magician never repeats himself, and you move on to another trick.

Required: A coin or key.

Preparation: None.

Degree of difficulty: ∗

Method one – the foolproof method.

Method one works every time – guaranteed.

## Performance
*Method one*

1 Stand facing your friend, and ask him to do what you do. Take a key out of your pocket and place it in one of your hands. Instruct him to do the same.

   Place your hands behind your back and begin to pass the key from hand to hand. Instruct him to do the same.

2 Hold the key in one hand. Any hand will do, as it doesn't really matter. But for the sake of explanation we will say that you have the key in your right hand. Instruct him to do the same. Point out that there is no possible way that you can tell which hand he is holding the key in.

3 Bring your hands out from behind your back, fists clenched, and bring them up in front of you at shoulder height, like a zombie, or the old Frankenstein monster. Instruct him to do the same. Now the knuckles of both of your hands are almost touching.

4 Tell him that you picked up his subconscious signals (or you read his mind, or you hypnotised him and forced his hand. Don't copy my patter. Use your own and it will sound a lot more natural.). Ask him to unclench the fist holding the key. He does so.

   Two things can happen now. He can unclench his right fist, or his left fist.

5 Case one – He unclenches his right fist. Bingo – that's the fist you have your key in. You unclench your right fist and show that you both had the key in the same fist. Point this out forcibly. Say: 'Do you believe in the power of coincidence?

That's amazing, neither do I. But here's something even more amazing. You put your key in your right hand, and so did I.' You have successfully read his mind and predicted which hand he would place his key in.

6 Case two – He unclenches his left fist.

Bingo – his left fist is touching your right fist. You unclench your right fist and show that your fist contains a key, just like his does. Point this out forcibly. Say: 'By an amazing coincidence, we have both chosen the same hand to put our keys in. You know what they say – great minds think alike. They also say that fools seldom differ.' You have successfully read his mind and predicted which hand he would place his key in.

As you can see, this trick works every time, just so long as you don't repeat it. That would give the game away. You will also notice that I gave some patter suggestions. Patter is what a magician says to sell a trick to an audience. It's the story of the trick, and it is vital. Don't fall into the trap of just telling an audience what you are doing – 'John has picked a card and put it back in the deck, and now I am going to find that card. See, I've found it.' That sort of patter demeans your audience. They are intelligent people, they can see what you are doing, so don't insult them by telling them the obvious. Try to make your patter interesting. And feel free to ignore the suggestions that I give. Magicians tend to use a lot of one-liners when doing tricks, and some of them can be quite corny. In the right setting a corny line will get a strong laugh, but don't overdo them. Find the lines that suit your personality. If you are naturally funny, go for the one-liners. If you are more serious, deliver a more sober patter. If you are a natural storyteller, make each trick a small story.

Now for another way of doing this trick. It allows you to repeat the trick, and it looks better than the first way.

### Method two – the mentalist's way

1 Stand facing your friend, and ask him to do what you say. Tell him to take a key out of his pocket and place it in one of his hands. Instruct him to place his hands behind his back and begin to pass the key from hand to hand.

2 Tell him to settle on one hand and hold the key in that hand, with the fists of both hands closed. Point out that there is no possible way that you can tell which hand he is holding the key in.

3 Bring your hands up from your sides, fists clenched, and lift them in front of you at shoulder height, like a zombie, or the old Frankenstein monster. Instruct him to do the same. Now the knuckles of both of your hands are almost touching.

4 Tell him to concentrate on the hand which is holding the key. Don't look into his eyes – he may try to deceive you by glancing surreptitiously at the wrong hand. Look at the tip of his nose. It will twitch slightly in the direction of the hand containing the key. Look out for this slight twitch, and you will be able to correctly tell him which hand is holding the key. This works nine times out of ten, and will leave an impression on the person you are doing it for.

The second method is no more difficult than the first, but on so many levels is a better way of doing the trick. But magic is like jazz, and you are the musician. Practise both methods, and then use the one that suits your personality or performance style.

# Matchbox monte

Three card monte, or the three card trick, is a fairground classic. A member of the audience is invited to find the queen, but each time his choice is wrong. Often a previous spectator (a stooge of the three-card-trick man) has won, so that inspires our hapless spectator to bet more and more on the game, until he is wrung dry, or the cops arrive and end the charade.

Magicians love the three card trick, but it doesn't have to be done with cards. Here's a version that uses three matchboxes.

Effect: You display three matchboxes, and put a coin in one. No matter how they try, the audience cannot find the one with the coin.

Required: Four matchboxes. Two coins.

Preparation: Before the performance put a coin in one of the matchboxes, and tape this to your left arm beneath your shirt or jacket sleeve. (An elastic band works as well as tape.) Put the other three matchboxes and the second coin in one of your pockets.

The reason for taping the matchbox to your left arm rather than your right is that you will be making some of the moves with your right hand, and you don't want the spectators to hear the coin rattle in the matchbox at the wrong time. This is called your props 'talking' and is always a mistake.

Degree of difficulty: *

**Performance**

1 Take out one matchbox and the second coin, telling the spectators that you will put the coin in the matchbox. Hold the coin at fingertips and pretend to place the coin in the box, closing the box. You really hang on to the coin, gripping it lightly with the slightly curled fingers of your right hand. This is called palming, and is not as difficult as you might imagine.

2 Put your right hand into your pocket and ditch the coin. Immediately take out your hand and the other two boxes. Place these matchboxes on either side of the one which the audience thinks contains a coin.

3 Explain to the audience that one of the boxes contains a coin. Pick up the middle box with your left hand and give it a shake. The audience will hear a coin rattling, and will assume it comes from the box. In fact it comes from the box taped to your arm.

4 Pick up the two outer boxes with your right hand and shake them. There will be no rattle. Explain that the two outer boxes are empty.

Pick a spectator and tell him that he has to keep his eyes on the box with the coin in it.

5 Move the boxes around rapidly at random, and after a few moments lay them out in a line. Don't worry about a rattle during this – the audience will expect it.

6 Ask the spectator which box contained the coin. He will point to one. Pick it up in your right hand and shake it. There will be no rattle. Then pick up any of the other two boxes with your left hand and give it a shake. It will rattle.

Invite him to try again. Again he will be wrong. Try it a third time, but don't go beyond this. Remember, less is often more.

7 Once you become confident at this trick, you can fool around a little and have some fun. You might have your spectator get the wrong box time after time, but have someone in the audience get it right every time. Or you could have everyone get it right all the time, and have one person get it wrong every time. A little experimentation will show you what works for you.

# Pen from matchbox

This is a quick effect, and quite startling. You take out a matchbox from your pocket, open it, and pull out a full-size biro. Use a regular plastic biro for this, rather than an expensive pen. People are suspicious of expensive pens – they may assume it is a magician's prop disguised as a pen. This is not so ludicrous. You can get pens that open locks, pens that go through banknotes, pens that hide motorised invisible thread reels. So don't give them the chance to speculate. Use an ordinary biro, and they will believe you can perform miracles.

Of course if you are performing for children, feel free to take a very showy magic wand from a small purse. It's the same trick with different props.

---

Required: A matchbox. A biro.

Preparation: Take out the inner tray of the matchbox and cut out a portion of one of the narrow sides, big enough to allow the tip of the pen to pass into the matchbox. Put the doctored matchbox in your pocket. Put a biro up your sleeve, holding it there with an elastic band.

Degree of difficulty: ✳

---

**Performance**
1 Take out the matchbox and tell the spectators that you keep a biro in it. Hold the box in the hand that has the biro taped to it. Manoeuvre the box so that the tip of the biro enters the hole in the end of the matchbox. Have the box close to your sleeve so that the biro is concealed.
2 Open the box and swiftly pull out the biro. By swiftly I do not mean like a gunfighter drawing fire at the OK Coral, but don't do it too slowly either. A firm and decisive move works best.

You can also use the same method to pull a magic wand from a matchbox if you are performing for children. But don't use magic wands for adults. We don't believe in them.

## Tap away

This is a lovely trick that can stop people dead in their tracks. It is also quite easy to do. A friend showed it to me, but I believe it came originally from Tony Spina, owner of Tannen's Magic Store in New York.

Effect: You put a coin in your hand and tap it with a biro. But the biro disappears instead of the coin. You find that the biro is now behind your ear, but the coin then disappears.

Required: A biro. A coin.

Preparation: None.

Degree of difficulty: ✳

## Performance

1 Place a coin in your left hand, then clench your fist to conceal it. Hold a biro, like a wand, in your right hand. Explain that you are going to use the biro like a magic wand to vanish the coin on the count of three.

2 Count *one* as you bring the biro up into the air in an arc from the clenched fist towards your right ear, then bring it down sharply, tapping your fist. Keep looking at your fist as you do this. If you look at your fist, the audience will.

3 Count *two* as you bring the biro up into the air in an arc and down again on your clenched fist, the same as before.

4 Now comes the first bit of magic. When you count *three* bring the biro up in an arc towards your ear, but in one smooth movement leave the biro lodged behind your ear and bring your hand down sharply exactly as if you were repeating the *one* and *two* counts.

5 Look bemused and confused, then tell the audience that the trick has gone wrong. The biro has disappeared instead of the coin. Show them that the coin is still in your fist.

6 There will be a ripple of laughter as they discover the biro behind your ear. If they do not discover it fairly quickly, you discover it.

7 While they are concentrating on the biro, casually drop your left fist and ditch the coin into your pocket. Reclench your fist.

8 Tell them you will try again. Tap your clenched fist with the biro. Open your fist to reveal that the coin has disappeared. Graciously accept their acclamation. This looks like a skilled use of sleight of hand, whereas it is really an exercise in misdirection – making them look in the wrong place while the magic is happening.

# Final thoughts

There you have some simple tricks to get you started. Enjoy them, practise them diligently before doing them for others, and have fun. You have taken the first steps towards teaching yourself magic.

# Six magicians who have changed the face of magic

## Magician 1 – Jean Eugene Robert-Houdin (1805–71)

Born in France, Robert-Houdin had a brief but spectacular career on the Parisian stage, dazzling audiences with his sophisticated salon magic. A brilliant mechanic, he invented several illusions and combined mechanics with flawless sleight of hand to create very memorable magic. He abandoned the Merlin robes in favour of formal evening wear, and got rid of the huge boxes and drapes that older magicians used to conceal their methods.

His fame grew after he published his memoirs, in which he described how his performance of a bullet catch in Algeria persuaded local rebels that European magic was superior to native magic. As a result their rebellion collapsed.

## Magician 2 – Harry Houdini (1874–1926)

Born Erich Weiss, Houdini was not a great magician, but he made up for this by his brilliant death-defying stunts and his superb showmanship. The King of Handcuffs could escape from anything, and that image of the small man who could overcome all shackles appealed to the common man in the early days of the last century. Houdini also exposed fake mediums, published a lot, and starred in some very silly action movies. This larger-than-life eccentric brought magic to the masses, and we all owe him a debt of gratitude.

## Magician 3 – Doug Henning (1947–2001)

Doug Henning, a likeable Canadian illusionist, defied tradition by wearing flower-power jeans and t-shirts on stage, and was a true artist in every sense of the word. His Broadway shows were spectacular, combining major illusions with music, dance, an impish grin and a wicked sense of humour. At the height of his fame he retired to devote himself to promoting the transcendental meditation movement. Then, in his early fifties, he announced that he was putting together another show. Unfortunately, cancer took him before that could happen.

## Magician 4 – David Copperfield (Still with us and still performing)

David Copperfield came on the scene in the mid 1970s as a young, good-looking illusionist who had a penchant for spectacle. His main claim to fame is that he went bigger than everyone else. While others were content to vanish an assistant, Copperfield vanished The Statue of Liberty as part of the 1976 bicentennial celebrations. He went on to vanish The Orient Express and a jet, as well as walking through the Great Wall of China and levitating across the Grand Canyon. His TV spectaculars are shown worldwide.

## Magician 5 – Valentino (Still with us and still in hiding from angry magicians)

This American magician is not popular among his peers, because he is the man who agreed to expose Magic's Greatest Secrets for a Fox TV special, which was shown worldwide. This was followed by several more exposure specials, which saw cherished illusions revealed to the public. Valentino said that he exposed the secrets to force magicians to come up with something new and fresh, and to promote the art. I believe him. And I know my bookings have increased because of the renewed interest in magic he sparked.

## Magician 6 – David Blaine (Still with us and still performing)

We live in a Pop Idol age, and David Blaine is the perfect Pop Idol magician – no spectacular talent, no personality, and he dominates the airwaves. The taciturn New Yorker revolutionised television magic when he started doing his street magic specials. Instead of the cameras concentrating on the magician, in the old fashioned way, they focused instead on the reactions of the audience. Suddenly magic became cool again.

# 02

## self-working card tricks

**In this chapter you will learn:**
- Simple but high impact card tricks
- How to cause someone's chosen card to turn over in the deck
- How to vanish an ace
- How to control someone's mind so that they pick the same card as you do.

The definition of a gentleman is someone who can do card tricks, but doesn't. Of course this is cruel to us conjurers, though I have to agree with its accuracy. Nothing bores a layman more than a succession of pick-a-card tricks – unless it is those tricks that seem to go on for ever, and involve endless dealing of small piles of cards. Tricks in which the magician mysteriously ends up with a royal flush, or the four aces, and the others end up with dud hands, are also a big turn off – but that still leaves a whole lot of great stuff.

When you learn card magic there are a couple of guidelines to bear in mind. You are trying to entertain, not demonstrate skill. So if there is a simple way of achieving an effect, and a complex way, don't disdain the simple way. Flash isn't always good. There are some card sharps who can do magnificent riffle shuffles, superb flourishes, and perfect card fans. They can make the pasteboards dance in their fingers, until their art becomes a display of dexterity. To my mind they run the risk of crossing the divide and becoming jugglers instead of conjurers. There is also another risk. If you have such fantastic control of the cards, will anyone be surprised when your tricks work? It's just what they would expect. But perversely a performer who appears a bit clumsy, who handles the cards no better than his audience, might be credited with tremendous ability for pulling off the same effects against the odds. Many experienced performers hide their skill, and I think that this approach has a lot going for it.

Never repeat a trick – and never, ever try to do the same effect for the same audience using a different method. You might think you are being clever, but you are only asking to be caught.

Practise, practise, practise, and finally never reveal a secret. There are two ways to reveal secrets. Some people just tell how it's done, and that is enough to get you thrown to the wolves in any company of conjurers. The other way is by not practising enough, and presenting tricks in such a sloppy way that the secret is obvious. This is a worse crime. Don't let yourself down by being one of the bad magicians.

But enough – let's get down to magic. In this section we will begin with some self-working card tricks. Self-working means that the tricks will work if you just follow the instructions. Self-working does not mean simple, juvenile, or not worth the effort. Some of the effects, such as Do As I Do, are classics, and every performer, even the most skilled, will include them in their repertoire.

Once you can do quality magic with cards, it will be time to learn the sleight of hand moves that make miracles possible. A number of the basic moves will be covered in a later chapter, followed by some advice on using those moves to invent your own tricks.

Before embarking on card magic it might be appropriate to consider a story about David Devant, one of the top British magicians at the end of the nineteenth century. A fan approached him and boasted that he knew 300 card tricks. David Devant replied that he knew eight. Of course he knew the secrets behind a great many more than eight, but he knew eight intimately – every nuance, every subtlety of patter that could enhance their entertainment value. Follow Devant's advice. Learn a few tricks well, rather than half knowing everything. Above all enjoy it, and that will help your audience enjoy it too.

## Turned over card

As a professional magician I use this repeatedly because it works. It looks like it takes great skill, but it doesn't. It's quick and it's startling. What more could you want?

---

Effect: A spectator picks out a card, then returns it to the deck. When you spread out the deck their card has mysteriously turned over so that it is face-down in the face-up deck.

Required: A deck of cards.

Preparation: None.

Degree of difficulty: ✳✳

---

### Performance

1 Take the bottom card of the deck and turn it over so that it is face-up instead of face-down. You can do this covertly while you hold the deck of cards, or you can do it before you begin, and have the deck in the box with the bottom card turned over.

2 Slowly go through the cards, face-down, and ask a spectator to pick out a card and show it to those around him. This is important – the more people that see the chosen card, the more people who will be amazed when you get the trick right at the end. And you would be surprised how many people don't even remember the card they chose. By having everyone

see the card, you eliminate the risk of the spectator looking at you blankly at the end of the trick when you reveal his card.

3 Casually let the hand holding the deck of cards fall to your side. When you bring it up again, turn it around so that the bottom card is now on top, and the top card is on the bottom. Now all the cards are face-up except the top card, which is face-down. But it looks to the spectator as if all the cards are face-down.

4 Ask the spectator to push his card into the deck at any point he likes.

5 Point out that there is no way you can know what card he picked. Look him directly in the eye as you say this. If you look someone in the eye, they will look you in the eye. And if they are looking you in the eye, they are not looking at the deck of cards in your hands. Magicians call this misdirection.

6 Casually drop your hand to your side again. When you raise your hand you turn the deck once more, so that it is right side up. All the cards are face-down except the spectator's card and the card at the bottom of the deck.

7 Slowly spread the cards from hand to hand until you come to the spectator's card, which will suddenly appear face-up in the deck. Be careful at all times not to flash the bottom card, which is also face-up.

A bit of practise with this trick and you have a gem. Use it regularly.

# Disappearing ace

This is a beautiful effect, and will gain you great credit for skill, even though it is quite simple to do.

Effect: Display the Ace of Clubs, Ace of Spades, and Ace of Diamonds. Put them back in the deck. The Ace of Diamonds disappears from the deck and is found in your pocket.

Required: A deck of cards.

Preparation: Remove the Ace of Diamonds from the pack and put it in your pocket. Put the other three aces at the top of the deck so that they are easy to find. Alternatively, you can look through the deck in front of the spectators and remove the three aces, if that suits your performing style more.

Degree of difficulty: ✳

## Performance

1 Explain to the audience that you would like to show them a trick with three aces, because every other magician does tricks with four aces, and you want to be different. Pick out the Ace of Spades, the Ace of Hearts and the Ace of Clubs, and display them with the Ace of Hearts in the middle. If you arrange the cards properly the Ace of Hearts should be upside down, so that the point of the heart is all that can be seen sticking up between the two black aces.

2 Tell your audience that you have three of the aces – spades, diamonds and clubs. As the audience only see the tip of the upside-down heart, they will believe it is the Ace of Diamonds.

3 Now turn the cards over and replace them in the deck, with the Ace of Hearts somewhere in the middle. Hand the spectator the deck to hold.

4 Announce that you will secretly steal one of the aces.

'I never much liked spades, because I have an aversion to hard physical work. So I think I'll steal the diamond' you say.

5 Make a mysterious pass over the deck, and smile smugly. Now ask your volunteer to go through the cards and see if the Ace of Diamonds is still there. Of course it is not.

6 Ask the spectator to reach carefully into your pocket. He will withdraw the Ace of Diamonds, much to his amazement.

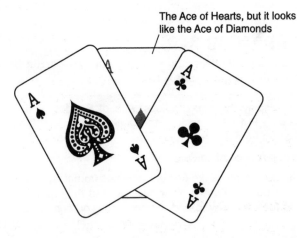

The Ace of Hearts, but it looks like the Ace of Diamonds

**Figure 2** Disappearing ace

# Double whammy

This little stunner is unbelievably easy – and unbelievably strong.

> Effect: A spectator puts an X on the face of any card. A second spectator puts an X on the back of any card. By weird coincidence they have both chosen the same card.
>
> Required: A deck of cards. A marker that is not working.
>
> Preparation: Get a marker and remove the top. Leave it aside for a few days until it dries up and no longer writes. Using a marker of the same colour, you put an X on the front and the back of one card and place this card somewhere in the middle of the deck.
>
> Degree of difficulty: ✳

## Performance

1 Ask two volunteers to help you. Give the first volunteer the deck of cards face-up, and ask him to put them behind his back. Tell him to shuffle the cards any way he likes behind his back.

2 Give him the marker that no longer works, and ask him to put an X on any of the cards, then shuffle the deck again.

3 Now give the deck to the second volunteer face-down, and ask him to hold them behind his back. He has to shuffle the cards any way he likes, and he too must put an X on the back of a card. Give him the marker to do this.

4 Take the cards back. One spectator has marked the front of a card, and one the back. Give the deck to the first spectator, face-up, and ask him to locate his card. He will pull out the card with the X on it. Put this on the table, face-up.

5 Hand the deck to the second volunteer face-down, and ask him to find his card. He will be unable to.

6 Finally ask him to turn over the card with the X on its face that is on the table. He will be stunned to find that his X is on the back – a coincidence of staggering odds.

# One ahead card

This is a nice card trick that is simple, virtually self-working and quick. It has everything you want in a card trick.

Effect: The spectator cuts the deck into three. Yet you can tell instantly what the top card on each pile is.

Required: A deck of cards.

Preparation: None.

Degree of difficulty: ✳

## Performance

1 Shuffle a deck of cards, then turn to a spectator and fan out the cards roughly, pointing out that all the cards are different, and they are not in any prearranged order.

2 When you fan out the cards, use this as cover to glimpse the top card, and remember what it was.

3 Square up the deck and put it down on the table, face-down. You now know what the top card is. Let's say it's the three of clubs.

4 Ask the spectator to cut the deck into three piles. While he does this make sure to remember which pile came from the top, and holds the top card, the three of clubs.

5 When the spectator has made his cuts, and has three piles of cards on the table, concentrate for a moment, then announce that the card on the top of one pile is the three of clubs.

6 Now take the top card off one of the other piles (not the three of clubs), look at it, smile, and put it face-down on the table, remarking: 'One down, two to go.' Remember the value of that card (let's say the ten of diamonds).

7 Stare at the cards for another moment, then announce that you know the value of another of the top cards, and it's the ten of diamonds.

8 Take the top card off one of the piles (not the one with the three of clubs, and not the one you have already gone to). Look at the card, smile, and put it down on the table face-down, saying: 'Two down, one to go.' Remember the value of that card (let's say the nine of spades).

9 Now announce that the final top card is the nine of spades. Take the card from the top of the remaining pile (it will be the three of clubs), and place it face-down on the table beside the other two face-down cards.

10 Repeat the names of the three cards – in our example, the ten of diamonds, nine of spades, and three of clubs. Then turn over all three cards. No one will notice the order of the three cards. All they will remember is that you got your prediction spot on.

# Do as I do

Magicians love Do As I Do effects. These are when you ask a volunteer to do the exact same things you do. Most of these effects finish with you accomplishing something, while your volunteer fails miserably. I can't say I particularly like that plot.

Do As I Do card tricks are entirely different. Here you do something and your volunteer does the same thing, and in the end you both end up having chosen the same card, against staggering odds.

The beauty of this is that it is easy, can be done impromptu, and is suited for one on one work, or for bigger groups. You could even get away with doing this one on stage, if you have a big enough personality. And that's saying a lot for a humble card trick.

---

Effect: You and your spectator shuffle, swap, and cut two decks of cards a number of times. You both pick a card. Remarkably both of you have chosen the same card.

Required: Two decks of cards, with contrasting backs. Most magicians use one red-backed deck and one blue-backed deck, though there is nothing to stop you pushing out the boat a little and using more exotic cards. This one can even be done with tarot decks. If you are chatting up a member of the opposite sex, it's a great way of showing you are on the same wavelength.

Preparation: None.

Degree of difficulty: ✳✳

---

## Performance

1 Show your audience that you have two decks of cards with contrasting backs. Call for a volunteer to come and stand at your left and help you.

2 Ask your volunteer does he believe in the power of coincidence. If he says yes, say that's an amazing coincidence. You do too. If he says no, just say the same: That's amazing. I don't either!

   Explain to your volunteer that all he has to do is follow your lead, and do as you do, without fail.

3 Tell him to pick up a pack of cards and start shuffling them. You shuffle the other cards.

4 As you finish shuffling take a quick look at the card on the bottom of your deck, and remember it. Let's say that the bottom card is the five of clubs.

5 You say: 'I have shuffled my cards and you have shuffled yours, so there is no way I could know the order that your cards are in. And you couldn't know the order my cards are in. So let's swap decks.'

You proceed to swap decks with your volunteer.

6 Ask your volunteer to pick any card from his deck, memorise it, and put it on top of the deck. You also pick a card and put it on top of the deck. But there is no need for you to remember what card you picked – it is completely irrelevant.

7 Now ask the volunteer to cut his deck. You cut the deck you are holding.

But unknown to the volunteer you have remembered the bottom card of the deck he is holding now (the five of clubs). When he cuts the deck, he brings that card on top of the card he has chosen and memorised a moment earlier.

8 Ask him would he like to cut again. Sometimes he will, sometimes he won't. If he does, you cut your deck as well.

9 Say: 'We have thoroughly mixed the cards, shuffled them and cut them. You take my deck, I'll take yours.' Now swap decks again. You are now holding the deck you began with, and you know that when you shuffled it at the start the five of clubs was at the bottom of it. So now the five of clubs is just above the chosen card of your volunteer.

10 Instruct your volunteer to look through the deck he is holding until he finds the card he chose. He is to place it face down on the table in front of him.

11 You go through the cards until you find your key card (five of clubs). Your volunteer's card will be the next one down. Take it out and put it face down on the table beside the card he has removed.

12 Briefly recap on what went on, saying: 'We both chose a pack of cards. We both shuffled those cards, and cut the decks. We both thought of a card, and put our selection on the table. You've heard it said that great minds think alike. I would draw comfort from that, except I know that fools seldom differ. Please turn over your card now.'

13 Your volunteer turns over his card. You turn over yours. They are the same. Holding one card above your head with one hand and the other above your head with the other hand, take your well earned applause.

# Torn deck – do as I do

I believe in simple tricks. You may have noticed that none of the card tricks described in this book involve dealing out poker hands or bridge hands. Unless something is direct and simple it lacks the punch to be real entertainment. The sort of card magic I like is quick-moving and snappy.

But occasionally something is so unusual that it is worth a bit of preparation in advance. I got this idea from an old effect described by Theo Annemann, a very influential performer and teacher, in a pamphlet he published in 1956. Although I did not like his effect, I liked the idea of tearing a pack in half. Thus I came up with the following, which illustrates the value of reading old material. Even if you don't get new tricks, you might start thinking in new ways.

---

Effect: The magician tears a deck of cards in two. He picks a card from one pile of torn cards. A spectator picks a card from another pile. Both cards match.

Required: A deck of cards.

Preparation: Unless you are unusually strong, the deck of cards must be placed in a moderate oven for an hour. This will weaken the cards sufficiently so that they can be torn in half easily.

Degree of difficulty: ✳✳✳

---

## Performance

1 Ask a volunteer to step forward and shuffle the deck of cards. Then ask him to cut the deck. He will cut the deck in the usual way.

2 Tell him that is not what you meant by cutting the deck. Pick up the deck and tear it across in half. There is a knack to tearing a deck of cards. If you grip one side of the deck firmly between the fingers and thumb of your left hand and the other side firmly between the fingers and thumb of your right hand, and push the top cards forward, you will find that you can begin by tearing the top cards, and as you continue to twist the deck between your hands, the tear will follow through the entire deck. Like pushing a car, it's all a matter of getting a good start. Keep twisting your hands over and back, and you will find that you can tear the entire deck. Of course, if you have left the deck a while in the oven, it is all that much easier.

3 Now ask the volunteer to take one half of the torn deck, while you take the other half.

4 Now go through the entire Do As I Do routine described earlier, just as if you had two decks instead of two halves of the same deck.

5 When you finally reveal that you have both picked the same card, and that the two torn pieces match perfectly, you will bring the house down. And deservedly so.

This is a trick that they will talk about afterwards. If you want to earn a reputation, it would be well worth your while experimenting with ovens and building up the strength in your digits. Press-ups on the tips of your fingers are what my karate instructor recommends, though he doesn't have to do magic with those fingers afterwards.

# Five places to do your first show

## Place 1 – A night out with your friends

For your very first performances stick to small tricks in a small setting. Learn a trick well and do it for friends while you are out together. If it goes wrong no harm is done, and if it goes right, you will want to show more and more magic. That is good. That is how enthusiasm builds up.

## Place 2 – A works get-together or family gathering

If your work colleagues are planning a night out, use it to show off. Do some tricks close-up, then grab the microphone and do something flashy like Cards Across or Bill in Lemon. You will be the talk of the night.

You can similarly hijack family events, such as 21$^{st}$ birthdays, grandad's 90$^{th}$, or a wedding or christening. You are among friends and family, so go for it.

## Place 3 – A variety show for a charity

Perhaps you belong to an organisation that puts on a show for old folks at Christmas? Volunteer your services for a five- to ten-minute slot. Maybe your child's school is fundraising, or planning a party in the classroom for Hallowe'en. They are looking for you.

You could just approach a children's charity, or the children's wing of your local hospital, and offer your services.

## Place 4 – A child's birthday party

If you have children, you know all about birthday parties. Every mum and dad would love someone to come in and entertain, if only for a few minutes. Start with your own children, or the children of friends, or children whose party your own children are going to. Just do a few minutes, and see whether you enjoy it. If you do, then go for it. You will always have a ready market. If you don't enjoy it, learn from the experience and try again.

## Place 5 – A talent show

Talent shows are very popular. Every pub seems to run one at some stage during the year. Often they are karaoke nights, but that doesn't matter. You will have a microphone, so do a trick. Magicians and variety acts rarely win talent shows, but they are often the act that goes down best with the audience. It's a paradox I've never been able to figure out, but that hasn't stopped me entering such shows whenever I need to break in new material.

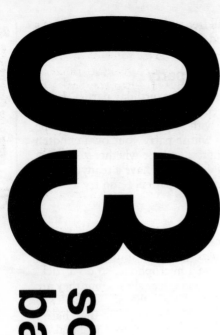

**03**

**some conjuring basics**

**In this chapter you will learn:**
- How to palm a coin or small object
- How to make a coin pass through a handkerchief
- How to make someone pick what you want him/her to pick
- How to make a change bag, which will change one object into another.

To win in the Tour de France you must first learn the basic skills of riding a bicycle. Similarly with conjuring, you must begin with the basics. In this chapter we will cover some of the basic moves and ploys that can be used to accomplish a wide range of magic tricks. In the next chapter you will learn the basics of handling a deck of cards.

Some of the basics, such as palming, are absolute essentials. Others, like Magician's Choice, are useful in their place. At the end of this chapter you will learn how to make a very useful prop – a change bag. It looks like a paper bag, but it allows you to switch small objects, or make them disappear. Make your change bag well and you will find uses for it. You will probably start inventing your own tricks.

That is one of the key points about learning the basics. If you go through all the moves in this and the next chapter, you may begin to think like a magician. And once you think like a magician, the rest falls into place.

There are very few tricks here, but many of the tricks further on in the book rely on the basic principles, so don't be tempted to skip. Skipping is for boxers, not magicians.

# Palming

Palming is the magician's word for secretly holding an item in your hand, concealed from the audience, while continuing to use your hand in the normal way.

There are dozens of different ways of palming, and some are highly specialised. They need the limberness of a concert pianist and an obsessive dedication to the art of sleight of hand. Other methods are quite easy, and permit a wide range of startling effects to be performed.

You can palm a wide variety of objects, from a complete deck of playing cards to a stack of coins, to a goldfish or a small mouse. T. Nelson Downes, one of the masters of coin magic in the golden age of vaudeville, was reputedly able to palm a stack of 40 silver dollars. I, on the other hand, have a life, and have never dedicated myself to the art to that extent.

Mastery of a couple of simple palms can take you quite a long way. We will start with small objects such as coins, keys or sugar lumps, then move on to playing cards. Small animals and fish I will leave to more specialised publications.

But before we begin, hold your hand up in front of you and look at it. Is it dead straight, like Bruce Lee about to deliver a finger strike? Probably not. Most of us hold our hands relaxed, with a natural curve and slightly bent fingers. So that is how you hold your hand when you have something palmed. The more natural the better.

### The classic palm
The coin is gripped between the ball of your thumb and the fleshy edge of your hand. Hold your hand slightly curved, with the fingers slightly bent. It is possible to hold two or three coins easily in this way.

### The finger clip
This is most suitable for coins and other small flat objects. The edge of the coin is gripped between your fingers. Your hand can be held by your side without the coin being seen.

### The thumb clip
The edge of the coin is pinched in the crock of the thumb.

### The finger palm
Hold your hand in a natural position with the fingers slightly curled. The coin should rest on the second and third fingers, with the curl of the fingers holding it in place. Another way of doing the finger palm is to grip the coin between the crease where your fingers join your palm, and the joints of your fingers.

### The back palm
This is an unusual palm, which allows you to show the front of your hand and your palm. You grip the coin between your index and little finger, with it hidden behind your middle and ring fingers.

Of all the palms the most useful are the classic palm, the finger palm and the thumb clip. One good way to practise is to have a number of coins in your pocket. Occasionally during the day reach into your pocket and pick out a coin, held in one of the palm positions. Try to hold it in your hand for the next five minutes while going about your normal activities. Remember this golden rule: if you look at your hands, then your audience will look at your hands. But if you forget about your hands and look elsewhere, that is what your audience will do too. If you can get used to palming a coin and then ignoring the fact that it is in your hand, you will quickly find that you can palm just about anything and get away with it. That's when the magic becomes easy and you can concentrate on the presentation.

# Coin vanish

This is a nice simple way of vanishing a coin, and is a good move to learn because though it is not a major trick itself, it can be used as part of a bigger trick. There are so many ways of vanishing a small object such as a coin, and sleight of hand experts will know several. But this one works as well as any other. You need a square of paper, roughly four inches by four inches, and a little bit of practice.

1 Place a coin on the square of paper, at the dead centre.
2 Fold one third of the paper down over the coin.
3 Fold the opposite third of the paper up over the coin. The coin is now in a tube of paper.
4 Fold one end of the tube down (closing one end).
5 Tell your audience that the coin is inside the wrapping of paper. To prove this rub the coin through the paper. The imprint of the coin will be left on the paper.
6 Now lift the tube up, with the open side in your fingers, and simply allow the coin to fall secretly from the tube into your hand. You hold the coin trapped between the folds of your last two fingers and the start of your palm. This is called the finger palm position, and is a useful way of concealing small objects. Don't try to hold your fingers out straight in an unnatural pose. Allow the fingers to curl naturally and they will hold the coin in place.
7 Now fold the final end of the tube down as if you were covering in the coin.
8 Point to the indent of the coin in the middle of the paper and tell your audience that the coin is now safely wrapped.
9 You can reveal the vanish any way you like. A good way is to reach into your pocket for a lighter or a box of matches, ditching the palmed coin as you do so. Take out the lighter and set fire to the paper pack and drop it into an ashtray. The paper burns through, revealing that the coin has vanished. **(This part of the trick should only be done with adult supervision.)**

# French drop

You have just seen how to use a small sheet of paper to make a coin disappear. Magicians use everything from magnets on elastic pulls to skin-coloured flaps concealed within their palms to vanish small items, but some rely on pure sleight of hand skill. The French Drop is a classic vanish of a small object such as a coin, key, marble, or dice. It's easy to learn and deceptive.

1 Hold the coin or key between the thumb and the middle finger of your right hand. Your palm is facing upwards.

2 Your left hand comes in front of your right hand to take the coin. As soon as the fingers of your left hand are covering the key pretend to take the coin, but secretly allow it to drop into your right palm, where it is held in place by the natural curl of your fingers.

3 Now close your left hand into a loose fist as if you had taken the coin into your fist. At the same time gently rotate your right hand so that your palm is facing in towards your body. This is a small, subtle movement that will prevent spectators seeing that the coin is still in the right hand. Do not move your right hand any more at this point.

4 Bring your left hand up and away, and follow it with your eyes. If you do this correctly the audience will be convinced that they have seen you take the coin from your right hand.

5 At this point you can close the fingers of your right hand to hold the coin in place, then point with your right index finger at the left hand, saying that you have the coin in your left hand. This is a natural movement that perfectly conceals the fact that the coin is in your right hand. Remember to hold your hand loose and relaxed. Nothing gives the game away more than fingers clenched so tight the knuckles are white.

6 Now take away your right hand. If you have done all this properly, and kept your eye on the left hand, ignoring the right, then the audience will believe that you have the coin here. You can slowly open your left hand to reveal that the coin has disappeared.

7 Now it is time to make the coin reappear. The simplest way is to say something about disappearing money getting right up your nose. Then pinch your nose with your right hand, allowing the concealed coin to fall from your fingers. This gives the perfect illusion that you have squeezed the missing coin from your nose.

Alternatively, you can reach up behind someone's ear. As you do this bend your index and middle finger and take the coin from your palm between these fingers. It's quite easy to do – a little practise will suffice. Now straighten your fingers as you reach the person's ear, revealing the coin. It will look like you plucked the coin out of their ear.

# Coin escape

This is a neat way of making a small object such as a coin, borrowed ring or pocket watch, pass through the centre of a handkerchief. You can do this openly as an effect in itself, or do it secretly as a way of vanishing a coin, to be produced somewhere else later. All you need is a large handkerchief or a brightly coloured woman's headscarf.

1 Take the coin and display it between the thumb and forefinger of your left hand.

2 Drape the headscarf over the coin, so that the centre of the scarf is on top of the coin and the rest of the scarf falls over your hand.

3 Through the fabric of the scarf grip the coin with your right hand and lift it up slightly from the thumb and fingers of your left hand.

4 Put the coin back in between your left thumb and index finger. But as you do so, secretly pinch a bit of the fabric of the scarf between the coin and your left thumb. This is the key to the whole move.

5 Now tell the audience that the coin is hidden in the scarf – and show them that it is underneath. Take the hem of the scarf at the front (fingers side rather than thumb side) and flip this over your hand so that it falls on the other side of the scarf, which is resting on your left wrist. This is to show the coin is still there.

6 Now comes the clever bit. Instead of flipping the scarf back over your fingers, you take both the front (which you have already flipped) and rear hem together and flip both forwards over your hand.

To the audience it will look as if you simply draped a coin, then flipped the scarf over to show the coin was still there, then flipped the scarf back. However, what you have really done, as you can see easily when you try this, is taken the coin from inside the scarf to outside.

7 Now, being careful not to let them see that the coin is outside the scarf, pull enough of the scarf over the coin to conceal it. Then give the coin a few twists. It will look like you are securing it even tighter within the scarf. In fact, you can put an elastic band over the coin, creating the perfect illusion that it is wrapped tightly in the centre of the scarf.

8 Now you have two options. You can tell the audience that the coin once belonged to Houdini and has an uncanny knack of escaping, then work the coin free of the silk and reveal it. Or you can secretly remove the coin, to reveal it later as part of a bigger trick.

# Magician's choice

Magician's Choice is a way of giving someone a free choice from among three to six items, and controlling the choice in a subtle way so that they end up picking the item you want them to pick. It can be an extremely strong tool for all sorts of mental and other effects, and can even be used for a version of Russian roulette. I will explain Magician's Choice for three objects, and some of the applications for it. You will need to know how to do a magician's choice if you want to do Bill in Lemon, a great cabaret effect described elsewhere in this book.

Required: Three items to choose from.

Degree of difficulty: ✳

## Performance

1 Place the three items to be chosen from in a line in front of you. The item on your left is 1. The item in the middle is 2. The item on your right is 3.

2 The Magician's Choice relies on a certain subtleness of language, so be careful how you phrase things. Let us say that the item you want to force is in the middle. Ask the spectator to point to one item (do not say choose one item).

3 If he points to the middle item, you tell him that the middle item is his choice, and the force is complete.

4 If he points to one of the other items, then tell him that he has just eliminated it. Remove that item, leaving two – the one you want to force, and the other one.

5 Tell him he now has a free choice between two items, and to place a hand (or finger) on one.

6 If he picks the one you want to force, remove the other one, and the force is complete.

7 If he picks the other one, tell him he has eliminated a second option, and remove that one. That leaves one, which by elimination is his choice. The force is complete.

You can use the Magician's Choice to force an item in any position in the line of three, just so long as you know where it is in the line. You don't have to put the force item in the middle.

# Tricks with the magician's choice force

## Mind-reading routine

Required: Three cards with shapes on them – a cross, a circle and a triangle are fine. Alternatively you could use three city names, three animals, or so on. If doing this for children you could use pictures of three animals. An envelope containing a copy of one of the cards. This is your prediction.

### Performance
1 Lay the three cards out and shuffle them around on the table, before laying them in a line. Once you know where the force card is, you are ready to go. By the way, you can have the cards face down if you like, to add to the tension.
2 Tell the spectator that you have made a prediction. You are going to try to use your psychic powers of telepathy to guide their choice of card.
3 Go through the Magician's Choice, forcing the person to pick the right card.
4 Ask them to open the envelope and take out the card inside. It will match their card perfectly. Play up the mind control aspect by staring at them occasionally as if you are trying to get inside their head.

## Children's routine

Required: Three bright colourful boxes. Two of the boxes are either empty, or contain something that a child could have no possible interest in. The third contains a small gift for the child, or some sweets. This can be a nice birthday party effect if two of the boxes are empty and one full to the brim of sweets for all the children at the party.

## Performance

1 Ask the birthday child to help you select one box.
2 Go through the Magician's Choice. Every time she eliminates one box, show that the box is empty.
3 When she comes to the final box, remind her that sharing is caring, and whatever is in that box is for her and all her friends.
4 Reveal that the box is full of sweets, and stand back so that you don't get hurt in the stampede.

## Russian roulette routine

Russian roulette routines are popular because they are dangerous. Some performers, like Larry Becker, have elaborate routines with revolvers and live rounds. Derren Brown devoted an hour-long television special to a very tense and gripping Russian roulette. In Ireland we have a bad history with guns, so my routine does not use a handgun. Jail time is a poor payoff for a magic trick. My version uses four exploding toilets. It has a slight problem in that it is not very portable.

The version that follows is portable, and quite funny. It's a great trick for a cabaret setting.

---

Required: Three identical blocks of wood, about three inches square. An egg. Using superglue stick the egg to one of the blocks of wood so that it is in the centre of the wood and cannot roll off. You also need three identical paper cups, large enough to cover the egg. You also need to mark the block of wood with the egg on it, so that you can identify it immediately. A good way is to put a small chisel nick on two corners, diagonally opposite each other. Or use a pencil and put a proper mark, just as long as it is not too obvious. That way a glance will tell you which block of wood has the egg on it. You also need a hammer.

---

## Performance

1 Call for a volunteer to help you. Display the three blocks of wood, one with an egg on it. Emphasise the mess of driving your hand through the egg. Now cover the three blocks of wood with the paper cups.
2 Move the three blocks of wood around the table a bit, then ask the volunteer to do the same. No one now knows where the egg is hidden – except you, as you use your hidden mark on the block to identify the one containing the egg.

3 Move into a Magician's Choice selection process. Ask your volunteer to point to one of the three cups. If he points to a safe cup, suddenly smash your hand sharply down onto the cup, crushing it.

If he puts his hand over the egg, tell him that this is the cup he chose. Push it aside, then bring your hand down sharply on the other two cups, crushing them. Remove the cup from the egg, and smash the hammer down on the egg, to show what would have happened had he chosen the wrong cup.

4 Proceed with Magician's Choice until you are left with the cup with the egg, and end the effect as above.

This is a funny routine. Irish magician Keith Barry took it one step further, by replacing the eggs with something much more dangerous, and smashing the spectator's hand down on the paper cups. Don't try to copy him – his version ratchets up the tension several notches, but some of his imitators have caused serious injuries to their volunteers. Putting someone in hospital is not a good way of getting repeat business. What you have here is a very good, totally safe version of Russian routlette, but do not do it unless you are absolutely certain you know which cup conceals the egg, or unless you know a good dry cleaner!

# Change bag

There are many devices that magicians use to achieve their effects. Some of them are displayed in the open. These are your props. They include decks of cards or piles of coins if you are performing intimate close-up magic. They could include giant cages if you are a stage illusionist.

Then there are the hidden apparatus – fake thumbs, elastic pulls up your sleeve and reels of invisible thread. Use these correctly and you can perform miracles. And no one ever sees how.

Then there is a third class of device. These are objects which people see, but which are not quite what they seem. An escape artist can use a straitjacket that has been doctored to make getting out easier.

The change bag is a device of this type. To the audience it is an ordinary bag, but the magician can use it to switch items, or make them vanish or appear.

Change bags can be bought from any magic dealer. They are usually made of plush velvet and have a wooden handle. They look vaguely medieval, and add a bit of colour to your act. But they have the drawback that they look like magicians' props. Most people don't have vaguely medieval velvet bags lying around their house. What they have are paper bags.

If you can turn a regular paper bag into a change bag, you have something that looks innocent, but which can help you do the impossible.

---

Required: Two paper bags. The best type to use is the type you get takeaways in – the square ones with handles.

Preparation: Cut one of the bags in two down the middle of both sides and across the front of the bottom. In other words you have taken the back and half of both side panels from one of the bags.

Put a strip of paper glue down the sides of both side panels of this cutout.

Insert the cutout into the other bag and square up the top of the cutout with the top of the back of the whole bag. Press the sides of the cutout firmly against the sides of the whole bag. This allows the glue to stick.

You now have an ordinary looking bag, but at the back is a secret pocket. Because the secret pocket is made from an identical pocket and fitted in properly, it will be invisible unless someone opens the bag and inspects it carefully.

---

You can imagine the possibilities. Have someone put a red scarf into the bag. Reach in and pull out a blue scarf from the secret pocket. You have changed red into blue. Change a five pound note into a ten pound note. Change a blank sheet of paper into a note from the spirits. Put in a blank birthday card and draw out a birthday card to the child you are doing a party for. Put in a long and greedy list to Santa, and pull out a reply saying you must be joking. A prop like the change bag is only limited by your imagination.

## Effects with a change bag:

### Forcing a number

1 To force a number on someone is simple. If you need someone to pick the number 27 for a trick, just write 27 on a number of bits of paper, and put them all in the bottom of the bag before your performance.

2 Display a pile of bits of paper to your audience, each containing a different number. Allow the audience to check that they are all different. Gather the pieces up and put them in the change bag – but put them into the secret pocket, not the main bag.

3 Allow a member of the audience to reach their hand in (have them turn away to do this, so that they don't see that they are reaching into a pile of 27s). They pull out a number, and it's the number you are forcing on them.

## Predicting a newspaper headline

This cracker of an effect is a great publicity stunt.

1 A week before your performance put a small wage envelope into an envelope, and send it by registered post to the organiser of the event that you are going to be performing at. Write clearly on the outer envelope *Do not open before performance time*. Phone the organiser to tell him the envelope is on the way, and must be brought unopened to the performance.

2 Tell the organiser to bring a copy of the newspaper of the day. Specify the newspaper – the trick falls flat if you predict *The Sun* headline, and he brings in *The Times*.

3 On the night of the performance, you look at the headlines on the front page of your agreed newspaper, and write them on a sheet of paper. Write one wrong headline, and include this as well. I will explain why in a moment. Seal this sheet of paper in a wage envelope identical to the one you posted a week earlier.

4 Place this wage envelope in your change bag, and you are ready for the performance.

5 When you are ready for the headline prediction (second last trick from the end is a good position) call the organiser to the stage. Ask him to confirm (loudly and into a microphone if you are working on a stage) that he received an envelope a number of days ago, and no one interfered with it.

6 Ask him to open the envelope and take out what is inside. He will take out the wage envelope. Take it from him and put it in your change bag (into the secret pocket).

7 Open the day's newspaper and chat about the headlines. Focus obviously on the headlines that you have correctly predicted.

8 When you are sure that your audience is aware of the real headlines, take the wage envelope out of the change bag. But

the switch has taken place – you have the envelope that contains the predictions. Give it to the organiser and let him open it. Tell him to call out your predictions.

9 As he calls out each headline, point out the corresponding headline on the paper. When he calls out the incorrect one look confused, then smile suddenly. 'Sorry', you say. 'I got a bit ahead of myself. That's next week's headline.' Strangely enough many will believe this.

If you do this as a pure publicity stunt, send an envelope to a reporter or a radio presenter, and just perform the rest of the routine one to one.

A word of warning is appropriate here – do this trick with a straight face. I am a great believer in comedy, but this is not the place for it. If you can really read minds, think of the power of that gift. It's not something you joke about. There is a certain somberness about this trick, and if you get the tone right it will be a knockout.

## Change bag childrens' routine

The change bag is such a versatile prop you can use it for adult cabaret, for children's shows and for publicity stunt miracles. This routine for children is just a suggestion. I first saw this done on a beautiful sunny day in a crowded park in Dublin. Three of us had been hired by the local authority to do magic for the afternoon. There were also bands, Barney the Dinosaur, and a Dracula look-alike called Paddy Drack. Dublin magician Joe Daly performed this as he strolled through the park and the children loved it. He used a traditional velvet change bag, but the paper bag one is every bit as good.

Preparation: You need three bits of light rope or lace of about a foot long, and one of three identical pieces which have been knotted together into a long length. I recommend the bright colourful laces used on sports boots. They are very visual, and they are less bulky than normal rope. Alternatively, you could use the special soft-core magician's rope you can get from a magic shop. Don't use the three-ply nylon rope you have in the boot of your car for emergencies. It is not suitable for magic, which is why we tow cars with it.

Put the three pieces of rope that are tied together into the secret pocket of the change bag. Put the other three pieces in the bottom of the change bag. You are ready to perform.

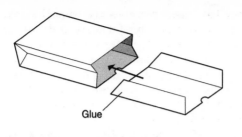

**Figure 3** Change bag

## Performance

1 Ask a child to help you. He has to hold his hands out and you will spill three ropes onto his hands. Holding the change bag in such a way that your hand is holding the secret pocket closed, you spill the three separate ropes or laces onto his outstretched hands. Don't worry if one or more of the ropes fall. Just call him a banana-head and tell him to pick them up.

2 Hold the change bag open (again using your hand to squeeze the pocket closed) and ask the child to drop the ropes in one at a time. As he goes to drop the first rope into the bag, suddenly whip away the bag and tell the children that he has put the first rope into the bag.

   Of course he hasn't, and he howls in protest.

   Call him a banana-head and tell him to put the rope in and stop messing – but whip the bag away again. Don't over do this, but do it enough to get the laughs.

   By the way, as you are clearly at fault, the kids are laughing at you, not at your helper. This is important. Never genuinely make fun of a child – it makes you the bully.

3 When eventually the child gets all the ropes into the bag, ask your volunteer to wiggle his fingers and do a magic dance. This will join the ropes together into one long rope.

4 Reach into the bag and pull out the three tied lengths. Hold the ropes over your head and take a bow with your volunteer, who has finally succeeded in getting the trick right.

# Five rules of professionalism (even if you are an amateur)

## Rule 1 – Be punctual

Being professional is not about taking the money. It is about acting in a professional manner. So be punctual. If you tell your next door neighbour that you will drop over at four o'clock to entertain her five-year-old and his pals, then be there at four. Not at five. Don't let the rest of us down by sloppiness.

## Rule 2 – Be consistent

Consistency is vital. If you decide to do shows, make sure that you give a consistent show. If you do an hour of magic in one house, then thirty minutes in the next house will not do. Word will get out that you blow hot and cold, and people will avoid booking you.

Consistency is vital when it comes to pricing. Decide on your price and stick to it. The best way of fixing your price is to find out what others in your area charge, and use that as a guideline. If people are charging £80 for an hour of entertainment at a children's party, you have two options. Charge £100 and try to build a reputation for quality to justify the extra money, or charge £70, and work on the principal of volume. Don't make the mistake of judging price according to a person's address. It's mean spirited, and it gets you a bad reputation.

## Rule 3 – Give value for money

This rule is equally true if you don't charge. It's a question of attitude. You must try to give the best show that you can. Don't even dream of charging for shows until you know that you can do all your routines, and present them smoothly.

## Rule 4 – Be reliable

Ask yourself a question. If you were booked to do a children's show for £80 and someone offered you £150 to do a different event, would you cancel the low paying show and take the better paid work? If the answer is yes, then close this book and take up crochet. You have no business studying magic. If you accept an engagement, then you fulfil that engagement.

I have a list of performers and phone numbers in my area, which I keep up to date. If I break a leg, I will be able to get someone to fill in for me, and no one who has booked a magician will be let down.

## Rule 5 – Look to your image

Pick an image for your performance, and stick to that image. If you do mentalism dressed as an Arab sheik one day and a gypsy fortune teller the next, you will be taken as seriously as you deserve to be.

But image goes far beyond your costume. Make sure your shoes are polished, your fingernails clean and your hair is washed. Brush you teeth before a performance, and if you are a man, shave. Your costume should be clean and your props in working order. If you remember all that you are sure to make the right impression on your audience.

# 04

## sleight of hand with cards

In this chapter you will learn:
- How to control the position of a chosen card in the deck
- How to make one card appear to change into another
- How to palm a card from the deck.

We have seen how to perform some quite good magic with no great degree of skill. Imagine what you could do with skill. That is the exciting territory we are going to explore now. Sleight of hand with cards is a huge field, with hundreds of books, videos and DVDs available on the subject. Some of the moves are breathtaking. A good card manipulator can show his hands empty and produce fans of cards repeatedly. The bad news is that it takes years to be that good. The good news is that it only takes days to master the basics and begin doing real skilled card work. In the next few pages you will learn how to force someone to pick the card you want them to, and how to allow someone to pick a card and put it in the deck, yet you retain control of that card and can retrieve it at any time. You will learn how to change one card into another, and how to palm cards from a deck without being spotted. You will have an arsenal of moves that will allow you to do many fine tricks. We will begin with what I consider to be the backbone of card magic, controlling a selected card.

## Overhand shuffle control

This looks exactly like the way everyone shuffles a deck of cards, but with a little practise it is easy to bring a chosen card to the top or the bottom, and keep it there.

1 The first thing is to hold the deck in the right way. Hold your left hand half closed with the palm up, and place the deck in it, with the faces down. The card faces rest across your fingers, while your thumb rests on the back of the top card.

   The deck should slope downwards to the left at an angle, with the cards resting along the palm and the bottoms of the fingers.

2 Now take a pile of the cards from the bottom of the deck between the thumb and middle finger of the right hand, and lift them clear of the deck. Bring this pile downwards over the other cards until its lower side touches your left palm. Press the left thumb against the top card of this pile, and simultaneously lift the right hand so that the card, or cards, pulled off by the left thumb, fall on top of the pile retained in the left hand.

3 Repeat this move until all the cards in your right hand have been shuffled off into your left hand, on top of the pile you are holding there. Pat the deck to smoothen it. As the overhand shuffle is normally repeated, it is essential to keep

the edges even, or you will end up doing the Texas shuffle – dropping the cards so that it takes us (Texas) ages to pick them up. That's a bad magician's joke, but you better get used to it if you want to hang around magicians.

Does it sound complicated? It isn't. If you have ever shuffled a deck of cards, then you can easily and smoothly do the overhand shuffle – and all that follows from it.

But remember: in doing the shuffle don't look at your hands or the cards. Make it a habit not to look at what you are doing, so that you don't telegraph your moves to your spectators.

The speed of the shuffle should be about the same as if you were shuffling the cards before a game of bridge, snap, or whatever it is you normally play. It should be neither too fast nor too slow, and the rhythm should remain the same throughout. You want it to look as if you are just shuffling a deck of cards, and to be honest that is all you are doing at this stage.

But with a little practise, you can control cards with the overhand shuffle.

## Controlling the top card

1  Hold the deck in the normal way in the left hand, and with the right hand take all the cards. But as you are drawing the cards up and away, with the thumb of your left hand draw off the top card only and leave it in your palm. This is the first move of the shuffle.

2  Without a pause or hesitation shuffle the other cards onto this one until the shuffle is completed. The top card is now at the bottom.

3  Again lift the entire pack and repeat the shuffle down to the last card – the card that was originally at the top and was then shuffled to the bottom. Drop this card on top of all the others in the final move of the shuffle. You have shuffled the deck and retained the top card in position at the top.

After a few attempts you will find this move easy to make. Practise this until it is automatic, and you can shuffle a card from top to bottom and back to the top again without hesitation and without looking. It should be so automatic that you can chat to your audience while you are doing the shuffle. Only in this way will you convince your audience that they are seeing a genuine shuffle.

# Controlling the bottom card

1 Hold the deck in the left hand and lift the lower half of the deck with the right to begin the shuffle.

2 In doing this press lightly on the bottom card with the tips of the left middle and ring fingers, holding it back. As you lift the pack with your right hand, the bottom card will remain in your hand, and will still be the bottom card.

3 Complete the shuffle in the normal way. The bottom card has now been controlled and kept at the bottom.

# Controlling the top and bottom cards

1 Hold the deck in the left hand and grip the deck with the right. Lift the entire deck up with the right hand, but press lightly on the top card with the left thumb, and the bottom card with the left middle and ring fingers. The top card will fall onto the bottom card and both will be retained in your left hand, while the rest of the deck is in your right hand.

2 Shuffle the cards in the normal way and finish the shuffle.

3 Pat the deck to smoothen the edges, then repeat the above move exactly as before, lifting the deck but leaving the top and bottom cards in place. Shuffle off the cards to the last card, which ends up at the top. If you check you will see that this has had the effect of keeping the bottom card at the bottom and the top card at the top.

Now we are ready to move on to real magic – controlling a chosen card to the top of the deck.

# Controlling a chosen card

1 Have someone choose a card, then begin to shuffle the cards in your hand.

2 When you have about a third shuffled casually tell your spectator to put his card back on top of the pile in your left hand. At this point make sure that all the cards in your left hand, including the spectator's, are fairly neatly squared up. If you are shuffling carefully this will be the case anyway.

3 Shuffle the next card onto the pile, but when you do, make sure it ends up sticking out half an inch from the others. Magicians call this protruding card an 'outjogged' card.

4 Shuffle the rest of the cards on top of the outjogged card, until all the cards have been shuffled.

5 Now you are holding the deck in your left hand, with the volunteer's card directly below the outjogged card. With your right hand you take the pile of cards directly under the outjogged card and pull them out, dropping them on top of the pile in your left hand. It's like a casual cut of the deck, and it brings the volunteer's card right to the top. Once you can do this smoothly, you can perform a wide variety of card tricks. It is probably the most useful card move of them all, allowing a spectator to put their card in the centre of the deck, and controlling it to the top of the deck.

## Forcing a card

Any method of giving someone a choice of cards, but really pushing one card on them, is a force. Learning to force a card on someone is a very useful skill. I will describe three forces, though dozens exist. Some, such as the classic force, are brilliant, but beyond the scope of this book. Others, which are sometimes found in beginner's books, are too juvenile to consider. The three that follow are simple but effective. If you are doing one trick involving a force, pick your favourite method and master it until it is very smooth. But if you are going to do more than one trick involving forces, vary the force you use.

## Riffle force

1 Hold the deck in your right hand, with the fingers at the top and thumb at the bottom. The card you want to force is on the top. The cards are face down.

2 Putting your left hand under the deck, use your left thumb to riffle down the top left corner of the deck. Tell the spectator to shout stop.

3 When they shout stop, stop riffling down the deck. You now have a break in the deck where they shouted stop. Shift your right hand so that it is gripping this new top section.

4 Put your left thumb on top of the top of the deck.

5 With your right hand pull away the top portion, but with your left thumb pull off the top card so that it falls down onto the bottom portion. This is the force card.

6 An audience might spot you doing this, so I always raise the deck up to eye level as I do it. I then hold out the bottom section, pointing to it and saying that is where the volunteer stopped me.

7 I ask them to take the top card of this bottom section, and memorise it. Of course I know exactly what card they chose, because I forced it on them.

## Cut force

This is another simple way of forcing a card, though this time you begin the force with the force card on the bottom of the deck.

1 Give the deck a shuffle but retain the force card on the bottom.

2 Square the deck and place it on the table, asking a spectator to cut the deck, putting the top pile to the right of the bottom pile.

3 Now tell him to pick up the bottom pile and put it on top of the top pile, at right angles to it. Now the cards are in an X shape, with one pile going up–down, and the other pile going right–left. The force card is at the bottom of the top pile.

4 Pause and make some remark that has little to do with the force. Comment on the trick you are about to perform, or make a joke of some sort. This breaks their concentration, which is important because the next step is the key, and you don't want them thinking too closely about what you are doing.

5 Ask the spectator to take the top pile of cards, and look at the card on the bottom of this pile. Tell him to remember it, then tell him to square up the deck and return it to you.

You have just forced the bottom card on a spectator, and if you do it with confidence, you will get away with it every time.

## Under the hanky force

1 Have the force card on top of the deck. Give the deck a quick shuffle but retain the force card on top.

2 Hold the deck in your left hand, face down.

3 Drape a handkerchief over the deck, but as you do this, secretly flip the deck over in your hand so that it is face-up.

4 Ask the spectator to grip the deck through the handkerchief and lift roughly half the cards up. The cards he picks up are face-up, though he doesn't know this.

5 Flip the half of the deck in your hands over again. It is now face-down again.

6 Ask the spectator to reach under the handkerchief and pick the top card from the pile in your hand.

7 As soon as he withdraws his hand, flip the cards over again so that they are face-up. Now ask your spectator to drop the pile he is still holding under the handkerchief back onto the pile in your hand.

8 Finally flip the deck over one last time so that it is face-down, and take away the handkerchief. If you have performed the sequence of moves correctly, he appears to have cut the deck under the cover of the handkerchief, and removed the top card from the bottom pile. In reality he has taken the top card of the deck, the force card.

## Double lift

The Double Lift is a useful card move which allows you to switch one card for another effortlessly. For example, you can show someone that the top card is an ace, and when they take it, it has turned into a completely different card. It's not that difficult to do, and a little practise will suffice to master this.

1 Hold the deck in the left hand, face downwards, almost in the dealing position. With the right hand square the cards at both ends.

2 With the tip of the right thumb lift the inner end of the top card and the second card about a quarter inch (0.5 cm) up from the deck. Hold this break with the pressure of your left hand fingers.

3 With your right thumb push the two cards forward as one, by about half an inch (1 cm).

4 Now hold the protruding end of the two cards with your right hand, and flip the double card over, resting it on the deck, but not letting it go. The audience will see the second from top card, but believe they are looking at the top card.

5 Now turn the two cards face down again, and square them up with the rest of the deck.

If you were to hand a spectator the top card now, he would be convinced that he had the card he had seen when you did the Double Lift, but he would have a different card. This useful sleight has many uses. A simple trick using the principal will be explained in the following chapter.

## Palming a card

Palming a card is not as difficult as it sounds, and it has its uses. It allows you to secretly remove one or more cards from a deck. They can later be reintroduced to the deck, or can be revealed in some other way.

The palmed cards are generally removed from the top of the deck, and that is the method that will be described here.

1 Hold the deck face downwards in your left hand. With your thumb push the top card out just a fraction (an outjog).
2 Bring your right hand over the deck and allow your fingers to rest along the protruding edge of the top card. In this position the palm of your right hand completely covers the deck.
3 Now press down with your fingers and the top card will pivot into your palm. Arch your hand slightly so that the card is gripped between your palm and your fingertips. Casually rest your hand there a moment, then move your hand very slightly to your right.
4 At the same time take away your left hand, holding the deck. It is a psychological fact that people follow the big motion. If you remove your right hand completely people will watch your right hand, and may see the palmed card. So you remove the deck, leaving your right hand in place. Then casually drop your hand to your side (keeping the palmed card hidden) or put your hand into your pocket if you want to temporarily ditch the card.

A word of advice – if you are putting a palmed card, or any palmed object, into your pocket, then do it naturally. The most natural way is to have a good reason to put your hand into your pocket. If you reach into your pocket and take something out, then you can ditch a card naturally. If you are not going to take something out, then leave your hand in your pocket for a few minutes, so that it looks as if you have a hand in your pocket, not as if you were putting something into your pocket. Use common sense and the magician's knack of misdirection will be yours.

# Final thoughts

You should now be able to control the position of a chosen card within the deck. You should be able to force someone to pick the card you want. You should be able to apparently show him the top card on the deck, then switch it. And you should be able to secretly remove the top card, or cards, from the deck, and reintroduce them there or elsewhere at will. You have an arsenal of good moves that will allow you to create your own effects. In the following chapter I will describe a number of tricks that are possible with a basic knowledge of sleight of hand. I will also give some pointers about creating your own unique tricks. But don't try them on the public until you are sure of your skills. Remember, the more you prepare the more you achieve in card magic, as in life.

# The five greatest magic tricks of all time

## Trick 5 – David Blaine's card through window

It is difficult to come up with something new. That is why David Blaine's card through window stands out. Someone picked a card and signed it, then Blaine threw the deck of cards at a window. The cards bounced onto the ground, but one was left stuck to the window. It was the signed card. But the real kicker was that it was stuck to the other side of the glass.

I will not say how it was done, but I will give a clue. An accomplice helped. Aside from that, you now have all the skills needed to achieve this extraordinary effect.

## Trick 4 – David Copperfield vanishing the Statue of Liberty

As part of the American bicentennial celebrations in 1976 David Copperfield vanished the Statue of Liberty before a small select audience and a worldwide television audience of millions. Now we know that the illusion was highly angle dependent, and it has been repeated by others. But Copperfield was the first.

## Trick 3 – Chung Ling Soo's bullet catch

Chung Ling Soo was not Chinese, but audiences in the early twentieth century believed he was. His most famous trick was catching a bullet in his teeth. It was a classic of magic, performed with a high degree of elegance. Unfortunately it is also one of the most dangerous tricks around, having claimed more than a dozen lives. And one fatal evening it claimed Chung Ling Soo, leaving a lingering mystery – was it a mistake, murder or suicide?

## Trick 2 – Derren Brown's Russian roulette

Russian roulette is a popular feat among mentalists, but none have done it quite as well as Derren Brown. He whittled thousands of volunteers down to one, then took him to a remote island with lax gun laws for the climax of the show. The tension was notched to the last, and the relief when Derren survived was palpable. There was controversy afterwards about the trick, but it remains the finest magic television special of all time.

## Trick 1 – the greatest – Peter Marvey's illusions

Peter Marvey is a Swiss magician who combines sleight of hand with stunning illusions. The greatest piece of magic I have ever seen – and this is an entirely personal choice – was an illusion he showed at the Blackpool Convention in 2002. He stood centre stage and put his right hand behind his back. He then pushed his right hand through his body until it came out his chest. He then turned around and followed his right hand, stepping through his own body and standing beside himself. Only it wasn't himself he was standing beside – it was a woman. It is difficult to describe and almost impossible to conceive how he did it. True magic.

**05**

**card magic
with skill**

**In this chapter you will learn:**
- How to use your skills to create your own tricks
- How to create laughter and mystery through unusual card revelations
- How to perform a true classic of magic – the Card Across.

If you use the tools you now have you can create your own brand of magic – once you understand what a card trick is. The basic plot of the classic card trick is that someone picks a card, and you reveal what that card is. But the more interesting you can make the revelation, the better the trick.

Consider the plot again. Step one is that someone picks a card. Here you have two choices – let them pick a card and then gain control of it, or force a card on them. Each allows completely different types of revelations.

If you let someone genuinely pick a card, then you need to gain control of that card using the overhand shuffle control. Once you have the card on top of the deck, then a number of options are possible. Some are easy. If you push the top card so that it sticks half an inch out of the deck, then drop the deck from a height of roughly a foot (30 cm) onto a table, the top card will be caught by the downdraft and will turn over and fall away from the rest of the deck. It's a good quick way of revealing a card.

Another option is to ask someone for a number. Holding the deck with your left hand, use your left thumb to pull back the top card (the selected card) and deal out the second card. Continue to do this as you deal off the right number of cards, finally dealing the selected card. It looks as if someone named a number, and their card was in that position in the deck.

Of course, if you are good at palming a whole range of new possibilities open up. If you palm off the selected card you can have that card found in your pocket, your wallet, your spectator's shoe, or even in a sandwich.

One lovely possibility is to palm off the card and give it to an accomplice who can conceal it beautifully. If you are doing this in a fast-food outlet, then have the selected card signed and shuffled back into the deck. Shuffle it to the top, palm it off, and pass it to your accomplice, who can insert it into the volunteer's burger. Imagine their surprise when you fail to find their card, and they turn back to their food. They bite into their burger, and find the signed card.

Another idea is for your accomplice to go into a nearby shop and tape the card to the inside of the window. You then throw the deck at the window from the outside, and one card sticks. The person who chose the card goes over to the window to confirm that the signed card is theirs – and finds it stuck on the other side of the window you threw the cards at. He will never forget that delicious moment of shock.

Of course you could go with a completely different approach. You could force a card on your volunteer. If you do that, then you have the advantage of having known well in advance what card he would choose. That leaves huge scope for the revelation. You could have a duplicate card baked into a birthday cake, or tattooed to your arm, or written in the clouds by a skywriter. You are only limited by your imagination. What follows are some of my simpler ideas.

# Rising cards

The rising cards is one of the real classics of magic. The effect is simple – a magician gets someone to pick a card. That card is returned to the deck. The deck is out of the hands of the performer, and the card chosen mysteriously rises from the deck. It is a very good effect, and there are many ways of accomplishing it, including invisible threads, pulleys and elastics. The following method will be found to work every bit as well – and has the advantage of versatility.

Effect: A spectator chooses a card, which is returned into the deck. The deck is put back in the box, and the selected card rises mysteriously out of the box.

Required: A deck of cards, and a good grasp of the overhand shuffle control.

Preparation: The box that the deck of cards comes in must be prepared in advance. The preparation is simple. Just cut a narrow panel out of the back of the box. The panel should be long and narrow, starting near the bottom of the box, at the middle, and going up three quarters of the way. Some boxes have the pattern from the back of the cards repeated on the back of the box. This is the best sort of box to use. When you put the cards into the box, the panel at the back is entirely concealed. You are ready to perform.

By the way, if you are going to perform with cards regularly, and are going to keep a deck in your pocket to be always ready for action, why not have a doctored box, so that you can do this effect at the drop of a hat?

## Performance

1 Ask a volunteer to pick out a card and show it to his companions. This is important – people have a terrible

tendency to forget their card, and that can put you in an embarrassing situation of 'Is this your card? I haven't a clue.' By asking others to look at the card, you guard against this, and against the danger of someone pretending that the card you reveal is not theirs, to embarrass you. People are bad-minded, and every magician has tales of being sabotaged like this. That is why you guard yourself against it.

2 Ask the volunteer to return the card to the deck and you give the deck a quick shuffle. Use the overhand shuffle control to bring their chosen card to the top of the deck.

3 Put the deck in the box. The top card is now against the back of the box, with the panel of the box matching the back of the top card. So the box looks innocent.

4 Hold the box in your right hand, fingers to the front and thumb to the rear.

5 With your left hand make mysterious rising gestures above the box. While you are doing this, put your right thumb on the bottom of the panel, and push the top card slowly upwards. After a little practise the tiny movement of your thumb will be unnoticeable.

6 When the card has risen half way out of the deck, reach down with your left hand and pluck it out completely. This will prevent your audience from noticing that it rose from the back of the box, not the middle.

7 Hold the card in front of your face, and take a bow.

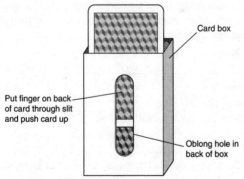

Card box

Put finger on back of card through slit and push card up

Oblong hole in back of box

**Figure 4** Rising cards

When displaying a card at the climax of a trick you can hold it anyplace – at waist level, above your head, to the side, in front of you. But top American magician Jeff McBride strongly recommends that you hold it beside your face. The face is the visible centre of your personality. It is what people focus on when they are talking to you. So by bringing the card beside your face, you are creating a frame for their appreciation of the trick. They are focused on the card – the climax of the trick – and on you, the performer of the trick. It is a natural applause cue.

If any of my tricks have a suitable climax – cutting and restoring a rope, finding a card, producing a silk – I always try to frame the climax like this.

# X-ray specs

This is a fun effect that shows how easy it is to create tricks if you know some of the basic card moves.

---

Effect: You have someone pick a card, but you are unable to locate their card. You put on your x-ray specs – and the card is written across them.

Required: A deck of cards. One pair of goofy sunglasses. An ability to force a card.

Preparation: Beforehand cut out two pieces of paper big enough to cover the lenses of the sunglasses. On both cards write the name of a card. I have 3 on the right lens, and clubs on the left lens of my glasses. Once these pieces of paper are glued to your glasses you no longer have functioning glasses, but you do have a neat comedy effect. Leave the glasses in your breast pocket and you are ready to perform.

Degree of difficulty: ✳✳

---

## Performance

1 Ask a volunteer to step forward and pick a card. Force the card on him that is written on your glasses.

2 Ask him to return the card to the deck and shuffle the deck thoroughly, before putting it down on the table.

3 Cut the deck and display a card, asking 'Is that the one?' If by some strange fluke you have got the right card (it will happen once in 52 goes) then take a bow and move on to the next trick. But if you pick the wrong card, as you hopefully will, act as if you don't care, and pick out another card.

4 After picking the wrong card two or three times, announce that you will have to use your x-ray glasses to do the trick.

5 Bending intently over the deck, remove your specs and put them on. If you are bent over sufficiently no one will see the face of the glasses.

6 Pick a few more wrong cards, then say that you will have to look deep into the eyes of your volunteer to get his card.

7 Straighten up and look directly at your volunteer – and enjoy the laughter as he sees his card written across your glasses.

# Identity crisis

This quick effect is a real stunner. All you need is two volunteers and an ability to do the Double Lift.

> Effect: Two volunteers select a card. On your command the cards change places.
>
> Required: A deck of cards and a good Double Lift. You also need one extra Ace of Spades.
>
> Preparation: Have the deck arranged so that the top three cards are Ace of Spades, Queen of Hearts and Ace of Spades.
>
> Degree of difficulty: ✳✳

## Performance

1 Call for two volunteers to help you, and have them stand one on either side of you.

2 Take out the deck of cards, remove them from the box, and put the box back in your pocket.

3 Do a Double Lift and show that the top card is the Queen of Hearts. Finish the Double Lift, then hand the top card to the volunteer on your right. She will think she has the Queen of Hearts, but really you have given her the Ace of Spades.

4 Have her hold the card sandwiched between her two hands, so that you cannot interfere with it.

5 Turn to the other spectator and do another Double Lift, showing her that the top card is the Ace of Spades. Finish the Double Lift and hand her the top card. She will believe she has got the Ace of Spades, but has really been given the Queen of Hearts.

6 Have her hold her card sandwiched between her two hands.

7 Now palm off the top card from the deck, and reach into your pocket, ditching the palmed card (so no one ever knows about the second Ace of Spades). Bring out the card box, and put the deck into it.

8 Turn to the first volunteer and ask her what card she is holding. She will say the Queen of Hearts. Ask the second volunteer and she will say she is holding the Ace of Spades.

9 Explain that with a clap of your hands, you can make the Ace jump over to the Queen, and the Queen jump over to the Ace, so that the two cards swap places.

10 Standing between your two volunteers, clap loudly once, then take a bow. Look up at the audience, as if you are wondering why you are not getting a standing ovation.

11 Saying, 'Don't you believe me?' you get your two volunteers to look at their cards. They have indeed swapped places.

# Card through hanky

This lovely effect looks like pure magic. It combines a number of skills you have been working on, including controlling a card and palming a card. But it is not too difficult to do.

---

Effect: A spectator chooses a card. The cards are wrapped in a handkerchief. The spectator names his card, and it mysteriously passes through the handkerchief.

Required: A deck of cards, a handkerchief, an ability to control and palm a card.

Degree of difficulty: ✳✳✳

---

## Performance

1 A spectator chooses a card and remembers it. The card is replaced in the deck and you use the overhand shuffle control to bring the card to the top of the deck.

2 Palm off the top card (the spectator's card) and retain it in your right palm. Keep your palm facing down, so the card won't be spotted.

3 Immediately take away the rest of the cards with your left hand, and take the handkerchief with your left hand and drape it over your right hand. This may take a bit of practise to do smoothly, but it can be done.

4 Under cover of the handkerchief turn your right hand over, so that the selected card is facing up. The card should be roughly under the middle of your right hand.

5 Place the rest of the cards on top of the handkerchief, right over where the selected card is, and aligned with it.

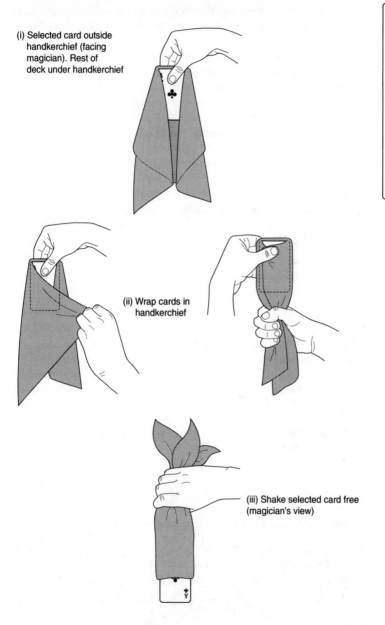

(i) Selected card outside handkerchief (facing magician). Rest of deck under handkerchief

(ii) Wrap cards in handkerchief

(iii) Shake selected card free (magician's view)

**Figure 5** Card through handkerchief

You now have to wrap the cards in the handkerchief, and if you do it right the deck is on the inside, but the selected card is on the outside.

6 With your left hand pull the portion of the handkerchief resting on your right wrist over the deck. Now with your left hand grip the deck, the handkerchief and the selected card tightly. You can take away your right hand.

7 You are now holding the deck at one end by your left hand. Using your right hand wrap the handkerchief tightly around the sides of the deck.

8 Now shift your grip with your left hand out slightly so that you are just gripping the handkerchief, not the cards. Immediately ask your spectator to name his card.

9 As he names his card, shake the handkerchief slightly and the spectator's card will fall free. It will look quite amazing, as the card will appear to pass right through the handkerchief.

This is a beautiful piece of magic with a stunning climax. If you are performing close-up magic it could be what you need to stand out from the crowd.

## Cards across

We end this chapter on one of the finest card tricks there is. It has everything – mystery, humour, audience participation. It works for all ages (except really young children) and it is quite easy to do. It can be done on a large stage or in a very intimate setting. And finally, there is no set-up involved. It can be done at the drop of a hat, as long as you or one of your spectators has a deck of cards.

Bill Malone, a top American professional, said that there are three classic card effects. This is one of them. The others are the Invisible Deck (a beautiful trick which can be purchased from any magic dealer) and Card to Ceiling, where a spectator-signed card ends up stuck to the ceiling of the room.

I first began to use Cards Across by accident. I had been hired to do a show in Abu Dhabi just a month after the September 11 terrorist attacks. At the time the climax of my adult act was a wacky version of Russian roulette with four exploding toilets. I knew that however difficult it would be to bring four toilets on the plane to Abu Dhabi, there was no way I was going to be allowed to bring the four explosives. So I had to find a new end to my act. I chose Cards Across, and I have not dropped it from my repertoire since. I hope you get as much fun out of it as I do.

As I describe this trick I will also describe the patter I use with it. You can do the same, or find patter to suit your performing style.

---

Effect: One person holds ten cards, while a second holds another ten cards. After some comic by-play, the first person discovers they now hold only seven, while the second person is holding 13 cards.

Required: One deck of cards and two chairs. The chairs are needed if you do this on stage – if you do it impromptu, then just change the presentation and leave out the chairs.

Preparation: Have one deck of cards, with any three spot (three of diamonds, three of clubs, etc.) in the 21$^{st}$ position. Have two chairs, one on either side of you, for the volunteers.

Degree of difficulty: ✳✳✳

---

## Performance

1 Call for two volunteers. Get a man and woman if you like. It offers scope for comic by-play. Have the woman on your left and the man on your right. Give the deck of cards to the woman and ask her to deal out ten cards into your left hand.

2 As she deals try to keep the cards roughly even in your left hand. When she deals out card number seven, allow the small finger of your left hand to rest on the edge of the seventh card. When she deals out the last three cards they will be slightly separated from the rest of the cards by your little finger. This is called holding a break.

3 A little bit of practise will show that it is easy to now cover the cards with your right hand and push the three cards up into your right hand, holding them palmed between the joints of your fingers and the heel of your palm. The cards will be bent, and if you don't move your fingers, they will stay there. Do this under cover of turning to the second volunteer.

If you don't feel confident holding a break, or if you are using a very old deck of cards that are not easy to work with, then there is another way of getting the three cards separated from the others, and it is simple. You just boldly count the cards to make sure that the volunteer has done this correctly. It is a simple matter to palm off three under cover of this count.

4 Place the cards in the left hand (now seven, though the audience thinks ten) on the chair at your right and ask the man to sit on the cards. Or else ask him to take out his wallet and you put the cards in his wallet. Ask him to sit on his wallet. While this is going on casually allow your right hand to hang by your side, so as not to draw attention to the fact that there are three cards palmed there.

5 Turn to the woman at your left and ask her to count the remaining ten cards into your left hand. You then, as you turn, casually bring your hands together and add the three palmed cards to this pile. Put the cards on the chair and ask the woman to sit on them. She thinks she is sitting on ten cards, but is really sitting on 13. Unknown to the audience the trick is done. But the fun is about to begin.

6 Tell your audience you are about to do a compatibility test – you will show the effects of a relationship on a man's wallet. It doesn't matter if the couple do not know each other. But if they are a couple the laughs will be intensified. I love doing this at weddings with the bride and groom.

Tell the audience that the man has put ten cards in his wallet. But you know the old saying – what's yours is mine, and what's mine is mine. When you get into a relationship the contents of your wallet seem to magically find their way into your girlfriend's petty cash account.

7 Go into the audience and ask someone to pick a card. Force the three spot on them using any of the forces already described in this book. Tell him that the card he has chosen will represent the number of cards that will jump from the man's wallet to the woman's pile of cards. He has chosen a three, so three cards will jump.

8 Turn back to your two volunteers and tell them that when you clap your hands they are to jump up as high as they can, then sit back down immediately, without scattering the cards. Clap your hands and the audience will howl with laughter as the two leap into the air.

9 Turn to the audience and tell them that the man is a little too enthusiastic. You will have to dampen him down slightly. Get a very good looking woman from the audience and ask her to sit on his lap.

10 When you clap your hands a second time the laughter will be even stronger, as the man tries to jump with the woman sitting in his lap. Clap a third time, and turn to the audience, announcing that the magic should have happened by now.

Ask the woman volunteer if she felt anything. If she says no, then turn to the male volunteer and make some remark about him not being up to the job, as she felt nothing. This sounds silly on paper, but an audience loves that sort of line. As the laughter subsides, thank the woman who has been sitting on his knee, and call for a round of applause for her as you allow her back into the audience. Then ask the man to stand up and take out his wallet, or pick up the bundle of cards he has been sitting on. Ask him to count the cards in a loud clear voice. There are only seven.

11 Ask the woman volunteer to pick up the cards she has been sitting on and count them in a loud, clear voice. There are 13.

12 Stand between your two volunteers and take a bow with them. Be gracious in how you handle your volunteers. You are gently poking fun at them, not demeaning them. Allow them to bask in the applause with you, and the audience will like you all the more.

There you have it – one of the best card tricks there is. If you do this smoothly it is a gem you will use all the time. Imagine a family gathering or a works outing that degenerates into a singsong. When your turn comes, do this trick instead. You will entertain them for ten solid minutes, and they will be talking about you long after the singers have been forgotten about.

# Five heckle killers

1 Stand over against the wall – it's plastered too.
2 There's one I hypnotised earlier.
3 Were you hit by a car recently, or were you born looking like that?
4 There is no point in responding to that heckle. It would be like taking a machine gun to a gnat.
5 Does your social worker know you're out tonight?

# Five things to say when a trick goes wrong

1 There's magic in my blood. It's a pity it's not in my act.
2 That's the first time it's gone wrong again.
3 If at first you don't succeed, maybe success isn't your thing.
4 There are days I wish I had kept the job at the abattoir.
5 It could be worse. My trousers could have fallen down.

# Five things to say when asked how you did it

1 Very well.
2 Lots of practise.
3 I could tell you, but I'd have to kill you.
4 Can you keep a secret? So can I.
5 Read *Teach Yourself Magic*.

# Five great one-liners

1 Ladies and gentlemen I am a ventriloquist. I talk a lot through my posterior.
2 Bob, make your mind blank. (Pause) That didn't take you long.
3 Did you see that trick? Good – the drugs have kicked in.
4 Don't sneer. I'm the best act in this price range.
5 Right now I'm having amnesia and déjà vu at the same time. I think I've forgotten this before.

# 06

## money magic

**In this chapter you will learn:**
- How to pass a coin through solid matter
- How to cause coins to vanish and reappear at your fingertips
- How to pluck coins from the air until you fill a bucket
- How to change wods of paper into paper money.

Those who say that money makes the world go around have a limited knowledge of physics. Gravity makes the world go around. Another popular misconception is that money can't buy you happiness. Of course it can, if you spend it on the right things.

Among magicians there is a misconception that coins were invented for us to do tricks with. It is simply not true. But that shouldn't detract from the joy of performing miracles with money.

The tricks in this chapter all use money. Most use coins, though there are some nice effects near the end that use paper money. Coin magic has a long history, reaching a peak in the vaudeville days with T. Nelson Downs, a superb performer who could enthral entire theatre audiences with the contents of his pocket.

It is unlikely that there will ever be another T. Nelson Downs, for the simple reason that entertainment moves on. Audiences are more sophisticated, and an act using coins, which cannot be seen beyond the third row, will not work any more.

Perhaps that is the appeal of coin magic. Since it is less commercial than most other forms of magic, it is done for love. That should be your attitude as you learn the tricks in this chapter. Do them for fun. There are some wonderful bits of magic here. Many are designed to be done seated at a table. So the next time you are in a restaurant with friends and everyone tosses in a pound for the tip, take the opportunity to try one of these tricks. It will add to the fun of your evening.

## Business card coin production

Tricks with business cards are always popular with magicians, because if you can use a business card for a piece of magic you can then leave your card with the spectator. It's by passing your number around that the calls will come in that turn your hobby into a money spinner.

This trick uses two cards. You can use playing cards, a beer coaster torn in half, or picture postcards. But I prefer to use business cards – my own. If you don't have business cards, you can get them printed cheaply. The easiest option is to go to any major shopping centre and use the quick-print machines they have there. Three pounds will get you 25 cards and you are ready for action.

Effect: Two business cards are shown. They are held together, and a coin drops from between them.

Required: Two business cards and a coin.

Preparation: Finger palm the coin before you begin the trick.

Degree of difficulty: ✳✳

## Performance

1 Before you begin, place a coin in your right hand, concealed in a finger palm position. The finger palm is a way of holding a coin covertly. You put the coin across your fingers, holding it in place by the natural curl of your fingers. For security the coin should be gently pinched in the fold of skin between your fingers and your palm. Now look around you. Nobody holds their hands rigid. Everyone has a natural curl to their hand. Many beginners make the mistake of trying to hold their hand straight, like a karate expert about to do a chop. But if you do this, you are only drawing attention to your hand, whereas you should be taking attention away from your hand.

   Say to a spectator that business is about making money. Ask to borrow his business card.

2 As he is getting his business card take your own card and hold it in your right hand. Slide the coin under the card so that it is concealed under it. You are now holding the card by the edge, between your thumb and your fingers, and the card hides the coin.

3 With your left hand take the spectator's card and brush it gently over your own card. Point out that there is nothing there.

4 Slide the spectator's card under your own card (but above the concealed coin). Now slide the coin so that it is hidden between the spectator's card and the fingers of your left hand. With your right hand brush the spectator's card with your own business card, and point out that there is nothing there.

5 Now place your business card under the spectator's card and under the coin. So you are holding two cards in an X shape with the coin sandwiched between them. Take away your right hand and make a mysterious gesture, then tilt the two cards in your left hand, allowing the coin to slide out.

6 Hand the spectator back his card and give him yours at the same time. Pocket the coin and tell him that's how magicians get rich. If you do this trick for a child (who obviously won't

have a business card) you can use playing cards, or two of your own cards. But don't pocket the coin – give it away. That's what magicians are expected to do with children.

# Travelling coin

This is a quick but neat effect that is perfect for a bar or a table. All you need is two coins. It is a real case of the hand being quicker than the eye.

Effect: You have a coin in each hand. Turn your hands over on a table and one coin mysteriously disappears, reappearing beside the other coin.

Required: Two coins.

Preparation: None.

## Performance

1 Begin with two coins. Put your hands on the table, palm up. Place one coin on the left palm, below the third and fourth fingers. The other coin goes on the right hand near the base of the thumb. Hold your hands about a foot apart on the table top.

2 At the same time turn both hands over so that the thumbs come close together. To the audience it will look as if you have a coin under each hand. In fact, because of the positioning of the coins, the one under the right hand will be thrown, and will land under the left hand. So you have two coins under the left hand, and none under the right.

   This happens automatically, but you still need to practise to get the timing right. And don't worry about being caught out. People see the big motion of the hands turning. Because of this they don't see the smaller motion of the coin going across.

3 Now tell your audience that you are going to test their powers of observation. Ask someone whether the coin under your right hand was heads up or tails up. No matter what they say they are wrong – it's not even there.

4 As soon as you hear their answer tell them they are mistaken – it is neither heads nor tails, because the coin got a notion into its head to high-tail it out of there. Lift the right hand to show the coin has gone.

5 Lift the left coin to reveal that the coin has travelled across.

The first time I did this for my wife, who is a professional magician, she gasped in amazement. Don't be put off by the simplicity of a trick. You might be surprised at the reaction you can get.

# Continuous coins

Any trick where you just produce coin after coin from thin air is bound to be a winner. This is an easy method.

> Effect: Coin after coin is plucked from an empty handkerchief.
>
> Required: A handkerchief (which can be borrowed). Twelve coins. A good knowledge of the finger palm, described earlier in the book.
>
> Preparation: Place six coins in your right-hand trouser pocket and six in your left-hand trouser pocket.
>
> Degree of difficulty: ✳✳

## Performance

1 Show clearly that both of your hands are empty. Take out the handkerchief in your left hand. Show that it is empty. Hold your right hand with all your fingers and your thumb together and pointing skywards.

2 Now drape the handkerchief over your right hand, with the centre of the handkerchief in contact with your fingertips.

3 Show your left hand to be empty, then grasp the centre of the handkerchief. Now turn your hands over so that the handkerchief is draped over your left hand, and your right hand is on top and outside the handkerchief.

4 Mime noticing something protruding from the centre of the handkerchief that is draped over your left hand. With your right hand mime taking this imaginary object and putting it in your pocket. Don't linger over this, or it will be obvious that you are holding nothing.

5 When you have your hand in your right trouser pocket finger palm a coin, then bring your hand out. If you get the timing right this will look like you have just put something in your pocket, not as if you have just removed something. As you bring your hand out, keep the back of your hand to the audience, so that they cannot see the coin held in the finger palm position.

6 Now you flip the handkerchief from the left hand over the right hand, so that the centre of the handkerchief corresponds to your upraised fingers. The audience do not know that you have a coin palmed in this right hand.

7 Once again you pretend to see an object in the centre of the handkerchief, and you mime taking it with your left hand and putting it in your left-hand pocket. While your hand is there you finger palm one of the coins.

8 Making sure not to 'flash' the hidden coin, take the centre of the handkerchief with your left hand, grabbing the coin that is hidden there as well. Now flip the handkerchief over your left hand. The coin will be revealed.

9 Take the coin in your right hand and put it in your pocket. But secretly finger palm it, and bring it out again.

10 Now with your right hand grasp the handkerchief (which is draped over your left hand) and flip it over your right hand. But as you grasp the handkerchief make sure to grasp the hidden coin too. As you flip handkerchief over, the coin is revealed.

11 Take this coin in your left hand and put it in your pocket, but secretly finger palm it, and bring it out again.

12 Repeat the lst seven steps a number of times. Do it a dozen times in quick succession. This is a trick that benefits from a quick pace.

13 Finally, discard the handkerchief and reach into both pockets. Pull out your hands, full of money. Bring your hands together and allow the coins to cascade down onto the table.

To your audience you have produced all those coins from bare hands and an empty handkerchief. If only they knew that only two coins are needed!

## Coin coaster penetration

This is a beautiful piece of magic that will get you credit for great skill. It is very visual and looks stunning. With a bit of showmanship and flair it is a miracle.

Effect: A borrowed coin (which can be marked) passes through a solid coaster and falls into a sealed glass tumbler – instantly and in full view.

Required: To do this trick you need a coin, a piece of paper, a glass tumbler and a bar coaster. If you can't find a coaster, a pack of cards, a small book, or a wallet will do as well. You also need to be able to do the paper-fold coin vanish described earlier.

Preparation: None.

Degree of difficulty: ✳✳

## Performance

1 Borrow a coin from a spectator. If you like you can get them to mark the coin. Some magicians love to have coins marked to prove that there was no trickery involving second coins. Others feel that the whole process of marking a coin slows down the effect and cuts into the entertainment value. It's a personal decision, and I don't bother having the spectator mark a coin, or sign a card, except in exceptional circumstances. If you do decide to have a coin marked there are a few ways of doing it. A permanent whiteboard marker works well on silver coins or polished copper coins (the shiny ones). Otherwise a small white sticker can be put on the coin and this can be initialled with an ordinary biro or pencil.

When you borrow the coin there is an opportunity for some impromptu comedy. You can open a man's wallet and comment on the contents. I often ask a spectator what he does for a living. Let's say he's a doctor. I then look in his wallet. If there is very little money inside (common enough in these days of credit cards) I may look at him pityingly and say, 'Being a doctor is more of a hobby than a career, I see.' It might not read funny, but delivered in the right setting, it gets a belly laugh.

Another idea is to ask for a loan of a two pound coin. If the spectator takes out a pound, take it from him. Say: 'I asked you for two pounds. You gave me one pound, so you owe me one pound. I owe you one pound. So let's call it quits.' You then pretend to pocket the spectator's money. This is not as strong as the first idea, but it creates the right comic atmosphere.

Whether you use these lines or not, always be on the alert for opportunities to draw out the entertainment value of an effect, as well as just performing the magic.

2  Place the coin in the centre of the piece of paper and do the paper-fold coin vanish. You end up with a piece of folded paper, which you place on the table, and a coin hidden in the finger palm position.

3  Pick up the coaster with the hand that contains the coin. You will find it very easy to slip the coin forward so that you are holding it under the coaster, with the coaster covering it completely.

4  Place the coaster on top of the empty glass tumbler. As you do this you make sure that the coin ends up between the coaster and the rim of the glass. The weight of the coaster holds it in place. And as the coaster is covering the glass, no one will see the coin.

5  Now tell the spectators you are going to perform a miracle right in front of them. Pick up the folded piece of paper (with the imprint of the coin still on it) and place it on the centre of the coaster. This is a good time to talk up the trick. This happens so fast that you don't want anyone looking away and missing the effect.

'Many magicians have made their reputation with the classic effect of coin through the table. But a table is a big bulky thing, and gives lots of room for cheating. I'm not going to cheat you people. I will do this right in front of your eyes.

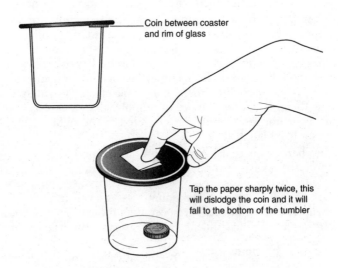

Coin between coaster and rim of glass

Tap the paper sharply twice, this will dislodge the coin and it will fall to the bottom of the tumbler

**Figure 6** Coin coaster penetration

I will push the coin through the paper wrapper, through the coaster, and into the sealed tumbler – and you can watch it all happen. To do this miracle I need to give the coin two taps – one hot, one cold.'

6 With this you tap the paper wrapper sharply twice (once if you do not use the gag about the hot and cold taps). This will dislodge the coin, which will fall to the bottom of the tumbler. It will look exactly as if you have tapped it through the solid coaster.

# Fan-glastic coin trick

This is a stunner. You not only vanish a coin, you vanish the glass that the coin was hidden under! It's not difficult to do, but practise this until it is so smooth that you can do it without thinking. This is one of those effects that must be done seated at a table, which limits its uses. But if you do this for the family at Christmas, they'll be talking about you until next Christmas.

---

Effect: Put a coin on the table and cover it with a glass tumbler. Not only does the coin disappear, so does the glass.

Required: You need a plain glass tumbler with straight sides, a borrowed coin, and a sheet of A4 paper or a good quality napkin.

Preparation: None.

Degree of difficulty: ✳✳✳

---

## Performance

1 Display the glass tumbler and tell your audience that this is the cleverest piece of engineering. If they knew what it really was, you'd have to kill them. It looks just like a tumbler, which is appropriate, since it is made of rare crystal. It is – and lower your voice conspiratorially when you tell them this – the power unit of the *Star Trek* matter transporter unit. You picked it up at a garage sale held by Scotty when he retired. Offer to show your audience how it works. Borrow a coin.

2 Place the coin on the table about a foot in front of you.

3 Place the tumbler on the table, upside down. Wrap the sheet of paper around the tumbler and twist the top around a number of times until you have formed a cover for the tumbler. Because of the stiffness of the paper it should be easy to push it firmly down until it takes the shape of the glass.

Make sure the cover goes to the table at all sides, and is moulded around the shape of the tumbler. The paper should be folded loosely enough to slide easily on and off the glass, but firmly enough to retain the shape of the glass, and to allow you to lift the glass away with the cover. While you are doing this explain that the CIA has been trying to find the crystal, and you don't like to leave it on show.

4 As you place the glass and paper cover over the coin tell the audience that we now have a working teleport device. Anytime you say beam me away, Scotty, the object within the transporter will disappear. As you are saying this make sure to perform the following action a number of times, in a casual way. With your right hand slide the paper cover up about half way off the tumbler, showing the coin underneath. Lower the cover again. Lift up the cover and glass together by gripping them firmly. Then swing your arm back so that the glass and cover come to the edge of the table, over your lap. Move your right hand forward again, and replace the glass and paper cover over the coin.

Do this casually a number of times as you talk about the transporter. Spectators will think that you are just showing them the coin, but really you are conditioning them so that when you make the crucial moves, they will not notice them.

5 Tell the audience you are now ready to show them the coin beaming away. Say in a deep authoritative voice: 'Beam me away, Scotty!' Then lift the tumbler and cover together and swing them towards the edge of the table as before. But as soon as it is over your lap, let the glass slide gently out of the cover, falling silently to your lap.

6 Look surprised that the coin did not disappear, and apologise to the audience. Tell them you will do it again, and place the cover down over the coin.

7 Now look around suspiciously. Tell them that sometimes CIA agents try to sneak in when you are showing off the crystal, and that triggers a defensive mechanism within the crystal. 'The last time this happened the coin stayed where it was, but the glass melted right away through the table,' you say, as you suddenly press down on the paper cover. The cover will immediately crumple, making it obvious the glass has disappeared. The audience will be stunned. Continue: 'The glass would have fallen to the floor but I caught it with my knees. I guess you could call it a knee jerk reaction.' Reach under the table and retrieve the tumbler from your lap.

8 Of course, this leaves the coin still on the table. Pick it up in your left hand and take it in your right hand (executing the French Drop move as you do this). To the audience the coin is now in your right hand, but it is really concealed in your left. Extend your right hand to the audience member who loaned you the coin in the first place, and hand him back his coin. As you open your hand the coin has vanished.

9 Make a joke of it. 'That's how we magicians make our money – by not giving back the money we borrow from volunteers. But it can sometimes get up people's noses – like this coin.'

Bring your left hand up to your nose and gently pinch your nose. As you do this allow the hidden coin to fall from your fingertips. It will appear that you have dropped the coin out of your nose.

Don't be put off if the routine seems to involve a fair amount of work. It does, but none of the moves are particularly difficult, and the plot is easy to follow. If you want to change the patter and make up your own, feel free. The *Star Trek* storyline gives a sort of lunatic's logic to what is going on, but any patter will do, just so long as you make it lively and interesting. Remember the golden rule – people are not interested in magic. They are interested in entertaining people performing magic.

## Coins across

This is a great close-up effect, and you will get credit for great skill. All you need to be able to do is to palm a coin well. One great way of learning to palm naturally is to put a coin in your palm and keep it there for the day. It's easier than it sounds.

Effect: You make two piles of three coins. But each time you pick up the coins, you find that one has jumped pile, until you end up with six coins in one hand, and none in the other.

Required: Seven identical large coins, such as a two pound coin, a two euro coin or an American dollar. The audience only ever see six of these, which is why it is important to be able to palm. This trick is done seated at a table, while your audience are sitting in front of you.

Preparation: Place all seven coins in your right trouser or jacket pocket.

Degree of difficulty: ✳✳

**Performance**

1 Reach into your pocket with your right hand and remove the coins. While doing this, centre palm one of the coins, so that you only put six coins down on the table.

2 Arrange the coins in two rows, one row coming out from your left, and the other row coming out from your right. The coin furthest away on your left is A. The middle one is B. The near one is C. The coin furthest away on your right is D. The middle one is E. The near one is F.

3 With your right hand (concealing the palmed coin G) reach over to the left and pick up coin A. Put it in your left hand. Pick up coin B and put it in your left hand. Pick up coin C with your right hand and put it into your left hand. While doing this allow coin G to drop into your left hand as well. You now have four coins in your left hand, though the audience thinks you have three. You no longer have a coin palmed in your right hand.

4 Close your left hand immediately so that the audience do not know you have four coins there.

5 Now with your right hand pick up coins D, E and F, but while you are doing this get coin D into the palm position.

6 Now close your right hand, and while you are doing this grip coin D in a palm position. Make sure to keep coins E and F slightly separated from D so that you can hold D easily when you release the rest.

7 Now make a slight 'throwing' motion with your right hand, and clink the coins in your left hand. Tell the audience that one coin has magically travelled from one hand to the other.

8 Open your left hand and drop the four coins onto the table, arranging them in a row. Open your right hand and drop the two coins (retaining coin D in the palm), and arrange them in a row.

You now have four coins in the row on the left, and two in the right.

9 Repeat the last six steps, cause a second coin to cross from the right to the left. You now have five coins in the row on your left, and one on your right. You also have one coin palmed in your right hand.

10 With your right hand pick up the five coins on your left and transfer them to your left hand, adding the palmed coin. Close your left hand over these six coins.

11 With the fingers of your right hand make as if to scoop the final coin into your right hand. What you really do is scoop

the coin to the edge of the table and allow it to drop into your lap. Pull your hand up and close your fist, as if you had the coin.

12  Now drop the six coins out of your left hand to the table, and open your right hand to show it empty. You have accomplished a miracle. The three coins to your right have mysteriously passed to your left.

13  Scoop up the coins, and as you replace them in your pocket, add the lapped coin, to leave you finished clean.

# Miser's dream

So many magic tricks use money you could be forgiven for thinking us magicians are obsessed with all that glitters. Not as obsessed as a miser. The following routine is the Miser's Dream – a bucket that is continuously filled with money.

---

Effect: The magician plucks endless coins from the air and fills a small bucket.

Required: A small tin bucket, such as the type children sometimes get at the beach. A stack of coins. A single coin, an elastic band and a length of fishing line. Thin fishing line works best.

Preparation: To perform the Miser's Dream you need a special gimmick. To make the gimmick, tie one end of the fishing line to the elastic band. Cut off about two inches of the fishing line, and glue the end of this to a coin with a dab of superglue. You have a coin attached to an elastic band by two inches of fishing line. Use a flesh coloured elastic band, and get the smallest one you can. Hook the elastic band around your right thumb and palm the coin at the other end of the fishing line, and you are ready.

Degree of difficulty: ✳✳

---

## Performance

1  Reach into your box of props. Slip the elastic firmly around the base of your right thumb. Slip the dangling coin into the palm position.

2  Take the stack of coins in your left hand and grab the bucket with the same hand. Hold the bucket by gripping the top of the bucket wall, not by holding the handle. From even a small distance it will not be possible to see that beneath your fingers are hiding a stack of coins.

3 Coming out towards the crowd, look upwards. The crowd will follow your eyes. Now reach up with your right hand and pretend to pluck a coin from the air. Really all you do is throw the coin forward from your palm and catch it in your fingertips. As it is attached by fishing line, this will be simple.

4 Display the coin at your fingertips, then put your hand into the tin bucket and pretend to drop the coin in. Really you just drop the coin and allow it to slap against the side of the bucket, creating the noise of it falling in. But because it is on thread the coin will snap back to you, and you retain it in the palm position.

5 Withdraw your hand from the bucket and continue to produce coins in the same way. Pull them from ears, from noses, from the air, from under people's chairs. The more ridiculous the place you find the coins, the more laughs you will get.

6 After producing a couple of coins, and hearing them clank against the tin bucket, you release a few of the coin stack in your left hand. You can now show that there are genuinely coins in the bucket.

7 Continue to produce more coins, and every now and again drop a few more from the stack in your left hand.

8 You will know when you have produced enough coins. When you have, release the final coins from the stack in your left hand, and slosh all the coins around in the bottom of the pail. Spill all the coins out onto the table. Take your bow, and as you sweep up the coins afterwards ditch the gimmicked one from your thumb into the pile of coins. You have just turned the Miser's Dream into reality.

Now it's time to abandon the coins and move on to magic with grown-up money, the type that folds.

## Bills from nowhere

This is a nice version of Flash appearance of a ribbon described in Chapter 07. But this time you are producing a roll of banknotes, and that is always a nice thing to produce. The only problem is that this must be an opening trick, because of where the money is hidden. You must be wearing a jacket for this, or a shirt or blouse with reasonably loose sleeves.

Effect: A magician pulls up his sleeves to show that he has nothing concealed. Yet he is able to produce a bundle of banknotes.

Required: A stack of perhaps half a dozen banknotes. You must be wearing a jacket, shirt or blouse with loose sleeves.

Preparation: Roll the notes into a tight tube and place the tube in the crock of your left elbow. Pull the fabric of the jacket or shirt over the notes to hide them. A slight bend in the arm will be sufficient to keep this bundle in place.

Degree of difficulty: *

**Performance**

1 With the roll of notes loaded as described above, face your spectators. With your left hand grasp your right sleeve by the elbow and yank it up to uncover your wrist, showing that your right hand is empty and there is nothing up your sleeve.

2 With your right hand reach across then grasp your left sleeve at the elbow and pull it back to show your left hand empty, and nothing up the sleeve. While doing this it is the most natural thing in the world to steal the notes and hold them between your fingers and the palm of your right hand. Be careful not to 'flash' the roll of notes to your audience.

3 Now hold both hands in front of you at shoulder height, with the left hand in front (to give maximum cover). Using the fingers and thumbs of both hands begin to unroll the roll of notes, so that the bundle of bank notes begins to appear at the top of your fingers.

4 After unrolling the notes half way, bring your left hand down, snapping them open fully. Fan them with your right hand to display them properly.

# Making money

This is yet another production of money trick. But tricks involving the production of money, even if it is just a coin from behind the ear, are always popular, because we are always searching for new ways of making money. This is a great effect, which can be done up close, on stage for adults, or as part of a children's routine. And you are producing far more than a coin.

A little bit of preparation is needed beforehand, and a good deal of practise to make it smooth. But this trick will more than repay that effort.

> Effect: The magician displays a number of blank sheets of paper. As he folds them over they turn into banknotes.
>
> Required: Four banknotes of the same denomination and four sheets of paper cut to the exact size of the banknotes. The larger the banknotes the more impact the trick will make, but even with fivers it is a good one. If you are performing for children, have the four sheets of paper taken from a comic book. If it is around Christmas time, use sheets of wrapping paper. If it is a corporate event, use the company's compliment slips. You get the idea.
>
> Preparation: Take all four sheets of paper and put them together. Fold the right-hand side in a third and the left-hand side in a third. Now fold the top down a third and the bottom up a third.
>
> Do the same with the banknotes. Now glue both bundles together back to back at the centre.
>
> Now open out the sheets of paper (leaving the banknotes folded). Take the top sheet of paper and put it to the bottom, underneath the bundle of banknotes. You are ready to perform. I normally leave this pile of sheets in my wallet, then take my wallet out and explain that I am so worried about being mugged that I no longer carry around paper money. Instead I just carry paper.
>
> Degree of difficulty: ✳✳

## Performance

1 Remove the sheets of paper from your wallet and hold them in your left hand. Take the top paper in the right hand. You now have the bundle in the left hand and one sheet in the right hand. Turn both hands over to show the undersides of the sheets. Because you have a sheet of paper under the pile of notes in the left hand, the audience sees nothing suspicious.

2 Take the second sheet into your right hand in the same way, then turn both hands over again, showing blank sheets in both hands.

3 Show the third paper but do not turn it over (it has a pile of banknotes underneath it!). Place it under the two sheets of paper in your right hand.

4 Now transfer the final sheet of paper from your left hand to the top of the pile of papers in your right hand. You now have a stack of four sheets of paper, with the bundle of banknotes underneath them.

5 Now fold the papers along the creases made earlier. If you hold the bundle at waist level and angle it correctly, the audience will not be able to spot the bundle of banknotes.

6 When the papers are in a tight bundle, turn it around in your hand (bringing the banknotes to the top) and unfold. What were sheets of paper are now real valid banknotes.

7 Casually move the top note to the bottom (concealing the bundle of papers) and transfer the notes to your left hand to display them.

8 Take the top note in the right hand and turn both hands over. Do the same with the second note. Push the third note under those in the right hand but do not turn it over. Finally, show both sides of the remaining note in the left hand, and place this final note beneath those in the right hand.

9 Fold the money and replace it in your wallet, warning the audience not to let the muggers know you have turned the paper into paper money.

## Final thoughts

In this chapter there were a number of coin and banknote effects. Some were easy, some required a bit of work. But any one of them, presented in an entertaining way, can be a winner for you.

Try them all, at least in rehearsal. Most can be performed with little advance preparation. All will help you develop the dual magical skills of dexterity and presentation that will make the tricks in the next two chapters, involving everyday objects, easy. Have fun with them, and don't be afraid to try them on your friends.

# Five rules of showmanship

## Rule 1 – Be larger than life

When you perform you are a magician, not a greengrocer. So act like a magician. Make no apologies for yourself. Be bold, be brave, and give it lots of energy. If you are shy, use the unusual situation of performing to allow yourself to drop your inhibitions and go for it. But remember that loud need not be brash, and always respect the people you are performing for.

Don't hide behind your magic, as some performers do. Instead use it as a tool to express your personality.

## Rule 2 – Know your character

Some people are quite happy being themselves, even when they are performing. If you are confident that your off-stage personality is the right personality on-stage, then try it that way. Just give a heightened version of your off-stage personality.

But many performers prefer to adopt a stage persona (even when just doing tricks around the dinner table). If this sounds better to you, then consider carefully what sort of image you want to portray. Have you genuine powers, or are you just a person to whom magic happens? Do you want to be funny or mysterious? Are you sharing with your audience or fooling them? Most of the top guys are sharing, not fooling, but you may want to go the other way.

Once you are happy with your magic personality, pick your tricks to suit that. If you perform for children, or do cabaret spots, your costume and props should reflect your on-stage personality. It's all part of the showmanship.

## Rule 3 – Use humour

Audiences love a laugh, and a good showman knows how to exploit that. When using volunteers handle them with a light touch. Be humorous and charming, rather than sneering and smarmy. If you look like you are enjoying yourself, nine times out of ten your audience will be enjoying themselves as well. Above all smile. Smile all the time. This is not a funeral, it is a show. Audiences respond to a smiling face.

## Rule 4 – Don't be afraid of danger

Harry Houdini was a lousy magician. All his contemporaries thought so. He performed in an era of greats, and his sleight of hand, his illusions and his thick guttural accent did not match the suave sophistication of his rivals. Of course you've all forgotten who his rivals were. Houdini rose above them through pure showmanship – and because he wasn't afraid to expose himself to danger. The hint of danger – the reality that he could die at any minute – drew the crowds.

You don't have to do this, but be prepared to take a risk in your magic. And I don't just mean the physical risks of routines such as Russian roulette or a Bullet Catch. Take a risk in your choice of material, in your handling of volunteers and in your performance style. Your audience will respond to the edge this gives your magic, and you will stand out from the crowd.

## Rule 5 – Rehearse

By now you should know the importance of practice and rehearsal. I have said it often enough. A famous magician once told me he could perform his act blind drunk. He never did, but he was that sure of his material. You need to be that sure too, both of your material and your presentation.

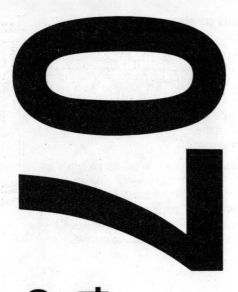

# 07

## tricks with ordinary objects

**In this chapter you will learn:**
- How to turn everyday objects into magic props
- How to perform miracles with whatever is at hand
- How to make a hanky come alive
- How to push a pencil right up your nose
- How to use elastic bands, bits of string, and sugar lumps to fool your audience.

This chapter is really just a collection of tricks and effects using a variety of objects, from elastic bands to rings to pencils. Some require skill, others don't. Some are complete pieces of magic; others are just throw-away effects. They are all included for the sake of completeness – any good conjurer should be able to entertain with whatever is around him, including the bits and pieces you would find around an office. Hopefully you will pick up something of interest in the following collection.

# Jumping elastic band

This simple trick can be done anywhere, with no preparation. All you need is an elastic band.

Effect: The elastic band is wrapped around two of your fingers, but jumps to wrap itself around your other two fingers.

Required: An elastic band and a hand.

Preparation: None.

Degree of difficulty: ∗

## Performance

1 Tell your audience that you have something special – an elastic band that Harry Houdini used to tie up all the money he made. Offer to show them a miracle.

2 Place the elastic band over the first two fingers of your left hand, near the base of the fingers. Hold your hand palm up.

3 With the other hand pull the elastic out across your palm, as you point out that the band is only over two of your fingers.

4 Turn your left hand over and close it into a fist. As you do this secretly slip the tips of all four fingers into the elastic band, then let go the band. Now, looking down, you can see your knuckles with the elastic band over the first two fingers. But if you were to look up, you would see the band cross over the tips of all four of your fingers. To the audience it appears that the band is only over the two fingers.

5 If you open your hand, the band will jump from the first two fingers to the last two fingers, which looks quite amazing.

6 Offer to show them the trick again, but this time tell them that you will make it more difficult, a real feat of escapology. Put the band over the first two fingers of your left hand again, but this time wrap the tips of your fingers tightly in an elastic

band, or use tape to bind your fingers together. This will make it impossible for the elastic band to jump, you tell the spectators.

7  Telling them that no restraints ever held Houdini, you now proceed to repeat the trick, exactly as above. Pull out the elastic band with your right hand, turn your hand over, let the band cross over the tips of your four bound fingers, then straighten your hand. The band will jump again.

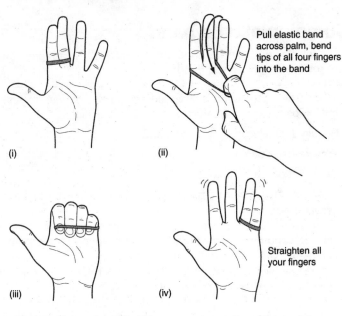

(i)

(ii)

Pull elastic band across palm, bend tips of all four fingers into the band

(iii)

(iv)

Straighten all your fingers

**Figure 7**  The jumping elastic band

It is rarely a good idea to repeat a trick. This little gem is one of the few exceptions.

## Flash appearance of a ribbon

Every good magician should be able to make things appear with a click of their fingers. This is a good way of making a silk handkerchief appear between your empty hands. It is instant, it is easy and it looks great. You can make a hanky appear, but the sort of long, narrow flimsy ribbons that women wear to tie up their hair are even better. They are multicoloured, and they allow you to move on to some rope flourishes after producing the ribbon.

This trick requires a long-sleeved shirt or blouse, a jacket or a jumper.

The only drawback of this trick is that it must be an opener – you cannot do this in the middle of a routine, as you will see.

Effect: The magician claps his hands, and a silk ribbon appears from nowhere.

Required: One silk ribbon, roughly 18 inches (45 cm) long, or a handkerchief.

Preparation: Take the hanky by the corner or the ribbon by the end and pleat it into a small bundle, using the kind of folds you would use if you were making a paper fan. Hold this bundle tightly and place it in the crock of your elbow. Pull some of the fabric of your shirt over the bundle to conceal it, then bend your arm to keep the bundle in place. You don't have to keep your arm bent at an unnatural angle – just keeping your hands up and gesturing with them gives you enough bend to hold the bundle. It doesn't matter which arm you use to conceal the bundle – use whichever arm feels right. A little experimentation will show you which one.

Degree of difficulty: ∗

## Performance

1 Make some remarks about being able to tell what someone does by looking at their hands. Make the sign of the cross with your right hand (you can do this even if you have the bundle concealed in your right elbow). Ask your audience what your job is. Someone will say a priest or a vicar.

Make another gesture – say a policeman directing traffic. Again ask what your job is.

2 Now sharply extend both your hands and clap your hands in front of your chest. This move straightens your arm, shooting the hanky or ribbon across your chest. As it was pleated concertina style, the ribbon will spring open. The effect is that the ribbon suddenly appeared as you clapped your hands.

3 With one hand grab the ribbon before it falls to the floor and wave it with a flourish. Say: 'If I did this with my hands, of course I'd be a magician.'

Alternatively, you can produce the ribbon by snapping forward just the arm that conceals the bundle and clicking your fingers. If you then grab the ribbon as it appears, you will seem to have clicked your fingers and produced the ribbon. It looks really neat.

# Tying a knot single handed

This is an ideal follow-up effect to the Flash appearance of a silk ribbon. It takes knack, but a little practise is all that is required. The ribbon you produced is held in your hand. You snap your hand and a knot appears in the ribbon.

A ribbon is ideal for this effect. But you can use a tie or a piece of string or soft rope instead.

---

Effect: You wave a ribbon in your hand and a knot mysteriously appears.

Required: A ribbon, lace or soft rope of roughly 18 to 24 inches (45 to 60 cm).

Preparation: None.

Degree of difficulty: ✳✳

---

**Performance**

1  Hold your right hand at chest level, palm upwards.

2  Put the ribbon across your fingers, close to your palm. One end of the ribbon should dangle down between your third finger and your little finger. The ribbon should run across your third finger, middle finger and index finger, and the other end should dangle down between your index finger and your thumb. The end dangling between your index finger and your thumb should be about eight inches long. We will refer to this as end A. The other end is end B.

3  Now turn your hand over so that your palm is facing down to the ground. Keep your little finger and your third finger together to hold end B gently in place.

4  Grip end A between your index finger and your middle finger.

5  Still holding end A, let end B and the rest of the ribbon fall from around your hand. As you raise your hand, holding end A between your fingers, the ribbon will fall naturally into a simple knot.

6  By raising your hand quickly the knot will tighten. Alternatively, just flick your wrist.

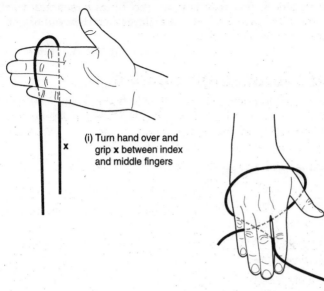

(i) Turn hand over and grip **x** between index and middle fingers

(ii) Slide rope from fingers to form knot

**Figure 8** One-handed knot

This movement is a smooth one. Begin by practising slowly, gradually speeding up. The important thing is not the speed but the smoothness. If you do this gracefully it is a neat flourish that will get a good reaction. I always make some remark as I do the flourish. I might say that since I started doing magic, knots keep appearing in my ties and shoelaces. Any light-hearted remark will do.

Please keep in mind that this is a neat flourish, not an amazing and mind-blowing piece of magic. If you present it as a dramatic miracle you will look like an idiot.

There is another way of flicking a knot in a piece of ribbon or rope. It will not work for a tie, but it is worth knowing in any case. It works well for an audience of children.

1 Tie a knot near one end of a rope or silk ribbon. Let us say the knot is at end A. Now hold the knot concealed in your right hand, with end B hanging down. Tell the audience that you are going to attempt to flick a knot onto the ribbon.

2 Give the ribbon a gentle flick and catch end B in your right hand, still holding end A and the concealed knot.

3 With a sharp flick you flick out end B, then look surprised when no knot appears. Tell the children that they will have to help you by shouting the magic word.

4 Now flick the rope again and catch end B. Tell the children to shout their magic word.

5 As they do this, you flick the ribbon again sharply. But this time you hold on to end B and let end A go. When the ribbon comes to a standstill they can see the knot, and assume you have flicked it onto the rope.

# Animated hanky

> Effect: Animated handkerchief – an ordinary handkerchief takes on a life of its own.
>
> Required: One handkerchief.
>
> Preparation: None.
>
> Degree of difficulty: *

## Performance

1 Spread the handkerchief open on the table. With your left hand grasp the top left corner of the handkerchief. With your right hand grasp the middle of the right-hand side of the handkerchief. Now lift the handkerchief and twirl it a number of times, so that it forms a rope-like shape.

2 Hold this 'rope' vertically in front of your body, with your right hand on top and your left hand at the bottom. Without letting go or loosening the twists, move your left hand up and grasp the 'rope' near the centre. Pull the handkerchief tightly between your hands, then gently release your right hand from the top. The handkerchief will stand, maintaining its upright position.

3 Pretend to pluck a hair from your head and wrap it around the top of the handkerchief. Now pretend to pull the handkerchief in various directions – and it will follow your pull. The secret is simple. By moving your left thumb and forefinger slightly you will be able to make the standing handkerchief tilt in any direction.

4 To end the performance have the handkerchief stand to attention again. Bring your right hand over the upright handkerchief, then quickly slap downwards, crushing the standing handkerchief.

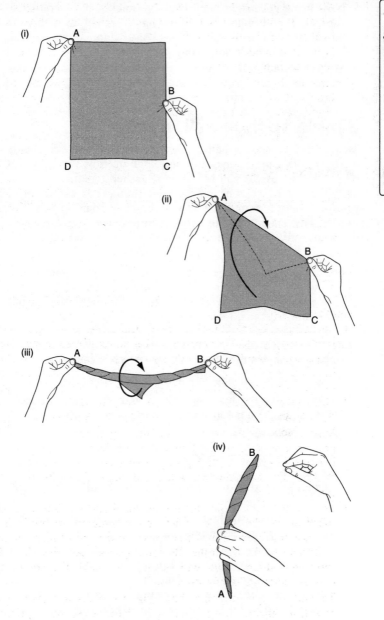

**Figure 9** The animated handkerchief

5 Now bring your right hand back up quickly, but secretly use the thumb and fingers to pull the handkerchief up with your hand. It will look as if you had slapped down the handkerchief and it flew straight back up.

6 Snap the handkerchief open to show no ropes, hidden springs or mirrors.

## Simple sponge ball routine

Magicians love sponge balls. These are small round balls made of super soft sponge. They can be folded up tiny, yet unfold to two inches across. If you hold two squashed together they will look like one. Most come in bright red, though you can get blue, yellow, green or orange if you search. They come in boxes of four at any magic or joke shop. Alternatively, you can make them yourself. Just get an ordinary bath sponge and cut it until it is roughly the size and shape of a golf ball.

There are as many sponge ball routines as there are magicians. My routine is simpler than most, because I feel that there can be a lot of repetition in many of the routines. My patter may sound childish, but trust me, I use the same patter for adults.

Effect: A red sponge ball becomes two, then disappears and reappears, then the two spawn a third – which is blue.

Required: Two red sponge balls and one blue sponge ball.

Preparation: Put the two red balls in your right-hand trouser pocket and the blue ball in your left-hand trouser pocket.

Degree of difficulty: ✷✷

### Performance

1 Tell your spectators that today is national head lice day – you read it in the papers.

2 As you say this casually drop your right hand into your right trouser pocket and palm one red ball.

3 Walk over to a woman with long hair and begin to pick at her hair. This keeps your fingers naturally bend and conceals the red ball. Then take up some of her hair in your left hand and drape it over your right hand, turning your right hand as you do so. The red ball is now hidden underneath her hair.

4 Tease the ball free, much to the amusement of the onlookers.

5 Announce that it is a head louse egg, and you can tell them because they are soft and spongy. Holding the ball in your left palm, press your right index finger down on the centre of the ball, as if you were going to saw it in half with your finger.

6 'As you can see, it looks like two eggs, but it's really only one', you say as you remove your index finger and allow the ball to resume its original shape.

7 Casually drop your right hand into your right trouser pocket again and palm the second red ball.

8 Pointing your index finger (which allows you to close your other fingers, concealing the ball) you repeat the last two steps, ending by asking: 'It looks like two, but it's really only ...?'

9 As the spectator replies one, you thank him for paying attention, going on: 'I'll do it one more time, just for the slow learners.'

10 This time you do not press your index finger down on the centre of the ball in your left palm. You quickly put the second ball down beside it and press your index finger down between the balls, the pressure of your finger concealing the fact that there are now two balls.

11 Say: 'It looks like two, but there are really only ...?'

12 As the spectator says one, reveal the second ball and tell him to keep up.

13 Put one ball in the right hand and pretend to take it into the left fist, executing a French Drop instead and keeping the ball in the right hand. Immediately pick up the second ball with the right hand and press the two together so that they look like one ball. To the audience you have a ball in each hand, but really the left hand is empty and the right has the two balls.

14 Give a flick of your left wrist, and mime the ball passing through your wrist, elbow, shoulder, and down the shoulder, elbow and wrist of your right hand. Open your left hand to reveal that the ball has disappeared. Open the right hand to show it has reappeared in that hand.

15 Now ask the original spectator to hold out her hand. As she does, casually reach into your left trouser pocket with your left hand, palming the blue ball.

16 Immediately count the two red balls into your left fist, keeping the fist closed to conceal the fact that there is a third ball hidden there.

17 Transfer the tight bundle of three balls into the spectator's hand and press her fingers shut tightly over them.

18 Now pretend to pluck a head louse from one of the men and drop it onto your spectator's outstretched clenched fist. Remarking that the male head lice, which are a different colour from the female, always manage to find a lady friend, ask your spectator to slowly and carefully open her hand.

19 As she does the third ball – which is a different colour – comes into view. It is a perfect climax to a short sponge ball routine.

I like this routine because it ends on a climax, it doesn't involve endless repetition of balls appearing in a spectator's hand, and the head lice theme allows for nice comedy. I hope you get as much fun out of it as I do.

## Pencil up the nose

If you are ever lucky enough to see a Coney Island freak show you will see amazing things. People who are just like you and me, except that they eat light bulbs, staple objects to their naked bodies, lie on beds of nails, dance on broken glass and swallow swords.

The freaky thing is that those stunts are genuine. Those people have spent years training their bodies and honing their skills to do things that we just weren't designed to do.

One of those things is the 'blockhead' stunt. This is when you get a six inch nail and push it up your nose and into your head. It's amazing to see, and relies on a little known quirk of anatomy. One of the sinus cavities is directly behind the nose, and if you gently push a thin object, such as a clean nail, straight in (not up) your nose, it will go into the sinus cavity. There is enough space there to completely hide a five inch nail. The rest is showmanship. You use a five inch nail, but tell the crowd that it is six inches long. And you can add your own touches, such as tapping the nail gently with a hammer. I even saw one performer use a drill, driving the spinning bit up his nose.

I am not going to tell you how to do that, and I recommend you don't try to find out.

The first time I performed the nail up the nose a friend who was a nurse lectured me at length about the dangers of infection. So I found a new way of doing the trick. Follow these instructions and you can drive a pencil up your nose without risk of infection, without using the sinus cavities, and without offending the nurses present.

Effect: You push a sharpened pencil right up your nose.

Required: A pencil or pen. Not every pencil will work. You need a longish pencil that is of uniform size, shape and colour all the way along its length. So avoid pencils or pens with writing on them.

Preparation: None.

Degree of difficulty: ✳

## Performance

1 Grab the pencil in your right hand at the eraser end. The pencil is pointing upwards, and you are holding it between the thumb and index and middle finger of your right hand.
2 Push the tip of the pencil up against your nostril. Hold your left hand by the side of your nose, with the index and middle fingers concealing the tip of the pencil. Those fingers also hold the pencil tip in position.
3 Now, miming pain and discomfort, slowly slide your right hand fingers up the shaft of the pencil. The end of the pencil slips behind your right hand and wrist.

As you continue to grimace (how would you really react if a pencil was going up your nose?) allow your right-hand fingers to slide all the way up until they meet your left hand. If you have done this correctly, it will look exactly as if you have shoved the pencil up your nose.
4 Now pause a moment, then begin to slip your right hand back down the shaft of the pencil. It will look as if you are sliding the pencil out of your nose.
5 Finally, pull the pencil clear and wipe it on a tissue, or on your sleeve if you want to be gross.

This is the correct way to perform the blockhead stunt, without being a blockhead about it.


# The rising ring

It is always a good idea to be able to take whatever is lying around and create mini illusions with them. This following effect takes a simple elastic band, but the effect is amazing.

Effect: An elastic band is stretched between your two hands. A ring placed on the band begins to mysteriously rise up from one finger to another.

Required: An elastic band, a ring, which may be borrowed, or a key.

Preparation: None.

Degree of difficulty: ✳

## Performance

1 Take the elastic band and snap it. You now have a length of rubber band, a few inches long. Thread one end through the ring, or the hole in the key.

2 Grip the elastic band in the middle with your left hand, taking the band between your thumb and index finger. Grasp the other end of the broken band in your right hand.

3 Stretch the band until it is taut. Now slowly raise your right hand until it is a couple of inches above your left hand. The ring or key will now be down by your left hand.

4 Stretch the band a little more, then slightly loosen the grip of your left hand. Slowly the elastic will begin to seep through your fingers. As it does, a bizarre spectacle unfolds. The ring or the key begins to ride up the elastic towards your right hand. It rises because the rubber of the elastic band has a high friction coefficient and grips it. Pure science.

5 A little experimentation will show how far you can go with this. If the band is the right length and the slope is right, this will look remarkable. As soon as the ring has risen far enough, or you have run out of elastic band in the left hand, bring both hands together, take the ring off the elastic, and hand it back. You can give out the elastic for examination, or as an unusual souvenir of an unusual performance.

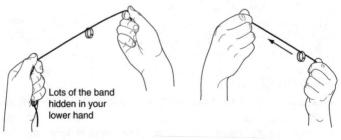

Lots of the band
hidden in your
lower hand

(i) From magician's viewpoint       (ii) From audience's viewpoint

**Figure 10** The rising ring

# Travelling sugar lumps

This is a nice trick that can be done impromptu with sugar lumps, small pebbles, marbles or similar items. I will assume you are using sugar lumps, as these are very easy to manipulate in this way.

I first came across this in Edwin Sachs' *Sleight of Hand*, published well over a century ago, and it is as good now as it was then. Before you do this trick try an experiment. Put a cube of sugar down on the table. Place your hand over the cube, positioning the cube so that it touches the base of your index and middle finger. Put a small bit of pressure down on the lump, then bring your hand up from the table, bending it slightly at the fingers. With a small bit of practice you will see how easy it is to take away the lump of sugar. This is a different way of palming from the traditional way of using the centre of the palm, but equally effective. More so in this case.

Having mastered the new palming technique, you are ready to perform.

Effect: Four sugar lumps jump from under one hand to another, until all four have gathered together.

Required: Five lumps of sugar, one of which is held in the palm position.

Preparation: Conceal one lump of sugar in your right hand.

Degree of difficulty: ✳✳

## Performance

1  Conceal a lump of sugar in the palm position in your right hand. Take four lumps of sugar and place them in a square shape on the table, about six inches apart. The upper left lump is A. The upper right lump is B. The lower right lump is C. The lower left lump is D.

2  Place your right hand (containing the palmed lump) over C and your left hand hand over D. Say 'lumps away' and lift your right hand, dropping the palmed lump as you do so. Lift your left hand, having pressed lump D into the palm position in your left hand.

You now have two lumps where C was and none where D was.

3  Place your right hand over B and your left hand over C, and again drop the lump from the left-hand palm position, while

picking up B in the palm position in your right hand, saying 'lumps away!'

You now have three lumps under C and none under D or B.

4 Place your right hand (with the hidden lump) over C and your left over A. Drop the hidden lump, while your left palms lump A. Taking your hands away you now have the four lumps gathered together at point C, and the trick is over.

5 You still have a lump palmed in your left hand. I just gather the sugar lumps up in my right hand, toss them into my left hand, and quickly toss all five lumps back into the sugar bowl. This may not be hygienic, but it ditches the extra lump.

If I am ever performing this effect for magicians, or for people who might try to guess how I did it, I always begin with a sugar lump of a different colour palmed between the little finger and the ring finger of my left hand. If I am using white lumps, I conceal a brown lump. At the conclusion of the routine I say: 'Of course, you all can guess that the only way to do that trick was with a fifth sugar cube.' Saying that, I drop the brown sugar lump onto the table beside the white lumps. I end with: 'What I can never figure out is why the extra lump is a different colour.'

# Five must-have props for the beginner magician (in order of importance)

## Prop 1 – A thumb tip

Every magician has a thumb tip. It is a fake thumb that fits over your real thumb, leaving a small bit of room. It is normally made out of plastic, but can also be aluminium. You can wear the fake thumb and even up close no one will suspect. It is used to vanish small objects such as silk handkerchiefs, bits of paper, the contents of a salt shaker, a cigarette or even a goldfish. It can also be used to make those objects appear. You can change a five pound note into a fifty pound note if you have a thumb tip, or you can use it to read minds. The possibilities are only limited by your imagination.

You will get a thumb tip, and all the other props suggested here, in any good magic or joke shop.

## Prop 2 – The invisible deck

This is my all-time favourite trick. I open my adult show with it, whether there are five or five hundred in the audience. The effect is simple – you ask a spectator to shuffle an invisible deck (great scope for laughs here) and pick a card. He then names a card and you remove a deck from your pocket. The card he names is turned over in the deck. It is entirely self-working and I get ten minutes of solid laughs, with a stunning climax, any time I use it.

## Prop 3 – Sponge balls

A simple sponge ball routine has been described earlier in this chapter. Lay people love this effect, and it fits easily into your pocket or purse. So make the investment. You will not regret the £2 spent.

## Prop 4 – A change bag

Change bags have been described in Chapter 03. If you are going to perform for children or in cabaret it is indispensable. It also has its uses in mentalism. The one you make yourself will be useful, but there is no harm in owning a colourful velvet one.

## Prop 5 – A dove pan

This is a flashy silver pan with a lid, rather like the domed lids waiters carry in the fancy restaurants. You light a fire in the pan, put on the lid, remove the lid, and the pan is full of doves, or sweets, or silk streamers or worms, depending on your audience and your performing style. A dove pan costs a bit, but it is showy and you will be a hit with your nephews and nieces if you can produce magic sweets with it.

# 08

# cabaret
# conjuring

**In this chapter you will learn:**
- The importance of showmanship and presentation
- Some sure-fire comdey ideas
- How to cut and restore a rope – and more
- How to produce eggs without a hen.

Don't be scared by the term cabaret. You don't have to be a star of stage to enjoy the tricks here. In fact, most of us never get the chance to perform in the ideal setting that a cabaret provides. But you can come close.

Any cabaret effect can be used in a variety of settings. Try these at your next office party. Or if you are at a wedding or anniversary reception and the band takes a breather, that's your opportunity. Jump in and show them some magic.

If you belong to a club that is putting on a fundraising show, or your child's school has a variety concert for Christmas, volunteer your services.

You might even put your name down for an open mike spot in a comedy club.

The effects in this chapter are all ideal in those settings – but don't limit yourself to these. Several of the effects in other chapters are equally suitable. One obvious one, from the card section, is Cards Across. Several of the effects in Chapter 09 on mentalism are also suitable. Book tests work well. So does Russian roulette.

In Chapter 10, children's magic, you will also find good material. The Linking Rings works as well for adults as for children. The card routine for kids can be modified to provide an entire cabaret spot for adults. Parts of the balloon material can also be modified. Performing cabaret is really performing to entertain. That might read like a tautology. Surely all performing is performing to entertain? Not necessarily. Some magic works by evoking a feeling of surprise and wonder. But in cabaret that is not enough. You must entertain.

That is why I love cabaret magic. It imposes a discipline on you. Not only must you be good, you must be good at being good.

# Five rules for cabaret magic

## Rule 1 – You must be good

Of course you should be good anyway. But if you are going to go on a stage in front of people, make sure you know exactly what you are doing. Double check that you have everything in place before you go on. Nothing is more embarrassing than attempting a cut and restored rope, and discovering the scissors are at home in the kitchen drawer.

## Rule 2 – Use humour

Humour always goes down well. Even if you are not a natural comedian, magic tricks lend themselves to a light-hearted presentation. The No Gag and the Baby Gag are obvious candidates. The Cards Across allow for great situational comedy. Don't take yourself too seriously, and the audience will take you all the more seriously for that.

## Rule 3 – Have a good opener

I had a judo coach once who told all his fighters to rush out and push their opponent off the mat. It might offend the judges, but it gets the respect of the opponent. Magic is similar. Grab their attention from the start. I come on with good instrumental music (not slow classics), blow a ball of flame, eat a balloon and crack a few good one-liners. It is a fast opening, and it puts me in charge of the audience.

An audience needs to know they are in the hands of a professional. Once they see you begin with confidence, they will relax and enjoy your performance.

## Rule 4 – Think about your image

Many pop and rock acts go on stage looking as if they are rejects from a Salvation Army or Oxfam shop. Ignore their example and dress well. My advice is to be the best dressed person in the room, but don't be overdressed. If it is a casual occasion, a good shirt and jacket are appropriate, and perhaps a tie. You could go for a fancy shirt or a bold tie if it suits you.

For a corporate event (if you are performing at a sales conference organised by your company) a good suit and tie is essential. But don't wear a tux unless your audience are in them.

## Rule 5 – Never turn your back on an audience

Many beginners (and some experienced performers) have a terrible habit of turning their backs on the audience to get props from their table. Any actor can tell you that you can pick up something without turning your back on people. Just think it out beforehand and be aware of the tendency. This is often enough to overcome it.

Another thing you need to do is to use the microphone correctly. A microphone is designed to pick up speech, not mumbles. It is designed to pick up a voice that is directed at it, not one from the other side of the stage.

In other words you speak into the microphone, not from two feet away, and you speak clearly.

Enjoy the magic.

# The No Gag and the Baby Gag

The No Gag and the Baby Gag are two classic bits of comedy that mentalists and magicians throw in for a laugh. They are great for MCs and comedians. Take this out at a party or in a pub, and you will be the life and soul of the gathering. Do these in a cabaret spot and you will bring the house down. And they are entirely self-working.

Effect: A volunteer is asked to try to predict the word you have written on the back of an envelope. He does so correctly – much to the amusement of the spectators. He is then asked to name any celebrity. You open the envelope to reveal a picture of that celebrity – and a big laugh.

Required: One envelope. One picture of a white baby and one picture of a coloured baby.

Preparation: Take the envelope and write *no* on one side of it. The envelope is now ready.

Take the picture of the white baby's face and the coloured baby's face, and glue them together back to back. The pictures can be photos, images taken from the internet, or simply drawings or cartoons you have done yourself. All that matters is that they are clearly baby faces, and one is white, one coloured. Put this combined picture inside the envelope. Place the envelope in a pocket with the *no* side inside, or place the envelope down on a table, with the *no* hidden. Now you are ready to perform.

## Performance
1 Pick on a volunteer in the audience and announce that you are going to train him to read minds. Ask him to make his mind blank. Pause for just a moment, then turn to the audience, saying: 'That didn't take him long.' It gets a laugh.
2 Ask your volunteer to look deep into your eyes. Again pause, before saying: 'But not like that.' You will get another laugh.

3  Announce that you are about to train your volunteer in the esoteric art of reading minds, then continue: 'We'll start with something simple. A simple yes or no answer will do. Can you tell me what word I have written on the back of this envelope?'

   Remove the envelope from your pocket and show it to the audience.

4  Your volunteer will say no. When he does, turn the envelope around and show that he has got the word right.

5  When the laughing subsides announce that you are going to try something even more impressive. Before you came out you put a picture of a well known celebrity in the envelope, because you knew it was the celebrity your volunteer would think of. Ask him to name any celebrity, and you have their picture in the envelope.

6  Let us say the volunteer picks Elvis Presley. Just open the envelope and show the picture of the white child.

7  After the laughter subsides, say: 'Last week someone tried to catch me out. They said Sammy Davis, Jr. But I was ready for them.'

   Saying this, you turn the picture to reveal the coloured baby on the other side.

The above routine may sound a bit silly, but don't ignore it on that count. It is a sure-fire winner with audiences. Even if you possess no comic talent whatsoever, you will get laughs with the Baby Gag.

# Eggs from nowhere

This trick goes a long way back with me. When I was 12 I was big – close to six foot tall and over 12 stone. So I could wear my uncle's tux when I performed. I can still wear my uncle's tux, because unfortunately I stopped growing at twelve.

I remember performing this trick in a local scout hall, and at the end putting the egg in the pocket of the tux. I forgot all about it. Many months later my uncle was wearing his tux at a fancy event. He put his hand into the pocket and a very rotten egg smashed. Luckily my uncle always had a great sense of humour.

Rather than upset relatives, I recommend you use a blown egg to do this trick.

Effect: You produce a number of real eggs from an empty handkerchief, then turn them into confetti.

Required: A blown egg and a real egg, a bowl or hat, a hanky and some confetti.

Preparation: To blow an egg is not difficult. With a scalpel or a pin, slowly put a small hole in the top of the egg. I normally drill the hole with the sharp point of a paper scalpel, though you can just push a pin through. Be careful not to crack the egg.

Now put another hole at the other end of the egg. Hold the egg over a glass or cup, and blow through one hole. The contents of the egg will shoot out through the other hole. That's your breakfast looked after. Now run the egg under a gentle tap to clean out the inside, and you have a blown egg.

Take the handkerchief and attach a short piece of thread to the centre of one of the sides. With superglue attach the egg to the other end of the thread. Now if you hold the handkerchief by the corners, the egg should hang around the middle of the handkerchief.

Now take your hat or bowl. Put the real egg in the bowl, and cover with confetti. Use enough confetti to cover the egg but not enough so that the audience will see the confetti. In other words, don't fill it to the brim.

Have the bowl on your table. Have the handkerchief on the table with the thread running from the handkerchief to the bowl. Have the blown egg in the bowl of confetti beside the real egg.

Degree of difficulty: ✳✳

**Performance**

1 Hold the handkerchief up by the lower two corners (the thread is on the opposite side). Display both sides. The egg remains concealed in the basket.

2 Lay the handkerchief half over the bowl with the top side (where the thread is attached) draped across the opening of the bowl. The centre of this side should be directly over the blown egg.

3 Show your hands empty, and pick up the handkerchief by the corners. Keeping the side stretched tightly between both hands, lift the handkerchief upwards and away from the bowl. Keeping the handkerchief stretched tightly prevents the blown egg from pulling down the handkerchief and giving the game away.

4 Now bring both hands together and gather both corners into your left hand, hiding the blown egg completely within the folds of the handkerchief. With your right hand take the other two corners of the handkerchief and swing those corners up to your right. Now you have the handkerchief folded into a pocket and held between your two hands. The egg is within that pocket.

5 Gently raise your right hand and shake the egg from the pocket, allowing it to land in the bowl of confetti. You have just magically produced an egg from an empty handkerchief.

6 After the egg lands in the bowl, toss the corners of the handkerchief held in your right hand onto the table. You still hold the handkerchief in your left hand by the two top corners.

7 With your right hand take one of the corners from your left hand and raise the handkerchief up again, keeping the side tightly pulled. The blown egg will come up from the bowl, hidden by the handkerchief.

8 Now repeat the fourth through to sixth steps, to produce another egg.

9 In this manner produce half a dozen or more eggs in quick succession. Do the first and perhaps the second slowly, but after that speed up the whole egg production.

10 When you have produced enough eggs (three is too few and 20 too many – the exact number only experience can tell you, as we all pace our performances differently) casually take the handkerchief (with the blown egg concealed within it) and put it away. Do not leave it on your table, where some curious troublemaker might be able to get it later.

11 Reach into the bowl which contains all the eggs you have magically produced, and pick out one egg. Really you are just reaching into the bowl of confetti and picking out the real egg. Break this egg into a glass to show that it is real.

12 Now pick up the bowl in both hands and approach your audience, as if you are about to throw the bowl of eggs at them. They will flinch as you approach, but instead of being covered in goo, they are showered with confetti.

Take your bow. Your audience will love this one.

This routine would make a great climax for a cabaret spot. You can talk your way through it, but it might be even better to do it silently to music. If you do, pick good lively music, something you can bop to. And don't leave a full egg in your jacket pocket!

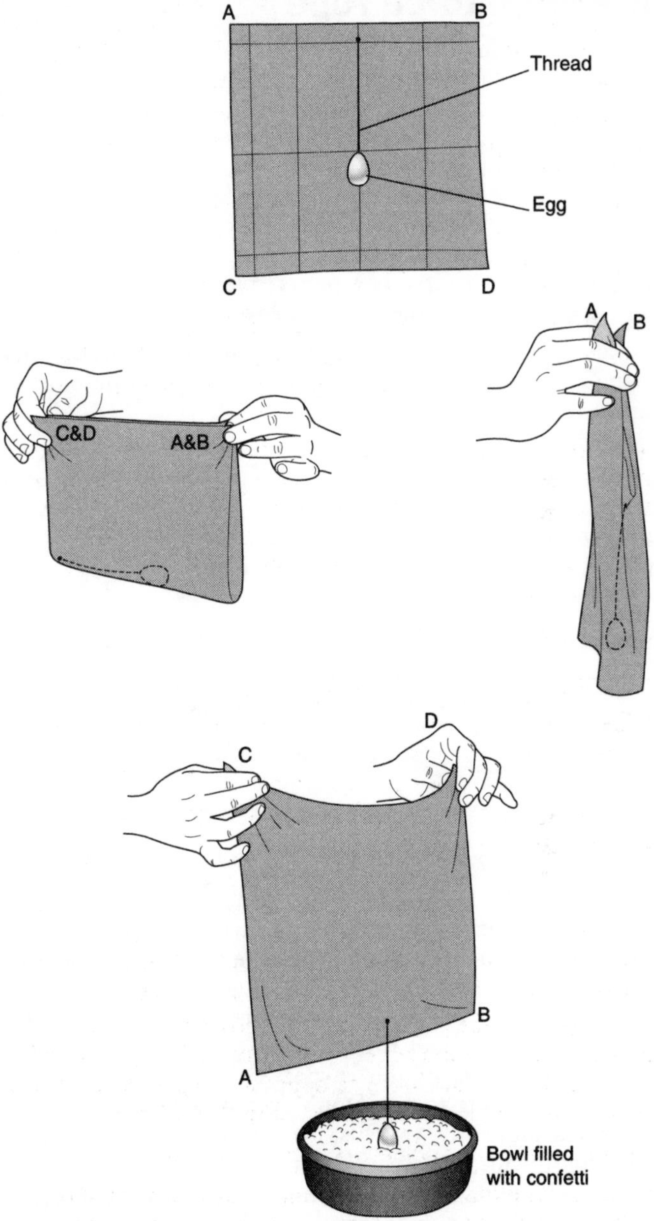

**Figure 11** Eggs from nowhere

# Cut and restored rope

The cut and restored rope is a classic, and like all classics it comes into its own when you put your own stamp on it. Many magicians have come up with elaborate variations on the theme. One of the best I saw was from Paul Zenon, who plays a lot of comedy clubs. He was telling gags into the microphone when he took out a pair of scissors and cut the mike lead. He continued to mime talking while he tied the ends back together. Finally, he waved his hands and restored the mike lead perfectly, and the sound came back on. It was a perfect piece, combining magic, timing, and acting, and the audience loved it.

I must also mention Penn and Teller, an anarchic American duo, performing a cut and restored snake routine. Gruesome but beautiful.

Here are two ways of doing the trick; pick your favourite. The first is for cutting a rope. The second is perfect for cutting mike leads or the cable to an electric light (if you have someone backstage to switch off the light when you cut the wire, and switch it back on when you restore the wire).

## Method one

Required: One length of rope, about three feet (one metre) long. One pair of scissors.

Degree of difficulty: ✳✳

In this effect you are cutting the final few inches off the rope, but making it look as if you are cutting the middle.

1 Display the rope, holding the ends between your left thumb and fingers. Allow the loop of the rope to dangle. Looking at the rope one end is near the crock of your thumb. The other end is out nearer the tip of your thumb. Look at this second end. Pick a spot about three inches (8 cm) below the tip of this end. In your mind this is spot X – the point on the rope that you are going to cut. Don't do anything with this spot. Don't mark it in any way. Just keep it in mind. It's where you are going to cut.

2 With your right hand bring the bottom of the loop of rope up to your left hand. To the audience what you are doing is taking hold of the centre of the loop, in preparation for the cut. But what you really do is different.

As you bring the bottom of the loop up, when it is level with your left palm, hold it there with the fingers of your left hand. The loop is held so that it runs over the rope a little above point X.

Now with your right hand pull point X through the loop and up level with the two ends of the rope that are just above your left hand. Doing this forms a small loop above your fingers. To the audience it is as if you have pulled up the centre of the loop, but as the illustration shows, you have just pulled up point X.

3  With the scissors cut through the rope at point X. You now have four ends. The ends of the long section are A and B. Those of the short section are C and D.

4  Hold on to ends C and D, and drop ends A and B. Your hand conceals the fact that you have a long rope looped about a short rope. To your audience you have two equal lengths of rope, having cut the single rope in half.

5  Now tie ends C and D together.

6  Holding the rope by one of the ends A or B, let the other fall. You now have a long length of rope tied in the middle. To the audience it is two lengths tied together.

7  With the scissors you can now trim off the knot by snipping away at ends C and D, making the knot smaller and easier to dispose of.

8  Holding the rope by end A in your left hand, grasp it a little below A with your right hand, and begin to wrap it around your left hand. As you reach the knot you will find that it slips along the rope easily with your right hand, and you can secretly slip it off as you finish wrapping the rope around your left hand.

9  Reach into your pocket for some magic dust to restore the rope. Under cover of this ditch the knot. Take your hand out empty but as if you were holding the magic powder. Sprinkle this imaginary powder over the rope, then unwrap it from your left hand to reveal that it is restored. Take your bow.

## Method two

Required: A rope or electric flex to cut. A small section of the same rope or flex concealed in your left hand. A pair of scissors or sharp knife.

Degree of difficulty: *

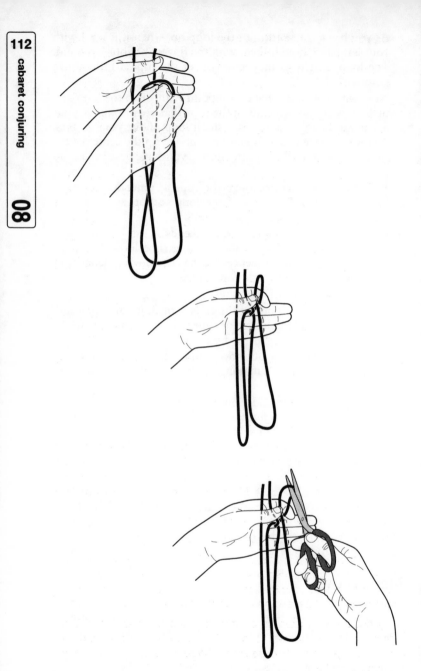

**Figure 12** Cut and restored rope – method one

1 Casually take hold of the rope or flex with your left hand. This is the hand with the hidden piece concealed beforehand.

2 With your right hand pull the hidden piece up in a loop and hold it above your closed left fist. It will look as if you have taken the rope and pulled a loop of it through your left fist.

3 With the knife or scissors cut through this section, and show the audience the two cut ends (really the ends of the hidden extra bit).

4 With your right hand grip both cut ends firmly, then, with exaggerated emphasis, blow on the rope. As you do this take away your right hand (and the two bits of the extra length).

5 With your left hand hold the restored rope or flex up, and look at it to draw attention to it. This is called misdirection – looking at something forces the audience to follow your eyes and look at it too. This gives you ample cover to put your right hand casually in your pocket or behind your back, and ditch the two pieces of rope it holds.

This second method of cutting and restoring a rope is simpler than the first. There are even simpler methods available, but some lack flexibility. There is never any harm knowing more than one way of achieving an effect. That gives you the creative flexibility to find the perfect method for your own personal style of magic.

# Three rope effect

This effect can be done with any thick soft rope, such as magician's rope, or with thick shoelaces.

Effect: You display three pieces of rope, then tie them together into one long length. You then magically removes the knots, effectively turning the three ropes into one.

Required: Rope or long shoelaces.

Preparation: With this one, it's all in the preparation. You do not have three equal pieces of rope. You have one long piece and two very short pieces. The long rope should be about three feet long (one metre) and the short ropes about four inches (10 cm) each.

Lay out the long rope on a table. Imagine an M with one end missing. This is the way to lay out the rope – up, down and up again. So you have two bends in the rope. Loop a short piece around each bend, as illustrated.

Now bring the two ends of the short piece together with the end of the long piece beside them, and tie these three into a knot.

Go to the other end and do the same.

You now have what looks like three ropes tied together at the top and bottom. This is all you need to do the trick. I will leave the patter up to you. When doing this for children I talk about a three-legged friend and his difficulties in finding a pair of shoelaces with three laces. I then do the trick. As you get familiar with the moves, I am sure that the patter will come to you.

Degree of difficulty: ✳✳

## Performance

1 Display the three ropes to your audience, then untie the knot at one end. You are now holding one end of the long rope and two ends of a short rope.

2 Tell your audience that you are going to drop one rope, and tie the other two together. Drop the long end, and then tie the two short ends together. It will look completely innocent, as if you had just tied two ropes together legitimately.

3 Now take the other knot, at the other end of the bunch of three ropes, and untie this. Again you are holding a long end and two short ends. Drop the long end and tie the two short ends together.

4 Now hold the rope up by one end. To the audience it looks like three pieces of rope knotted together – they can even see the knots. But really it is one long rope with two short pieces tied together.

5 Say: 'There you have it – three short pieces of rope turned into one long piece by the power of magic. Of course, cynics among you may wonder why, if I am a magician, I had to use knots. The fact is I have a talent for knots – I do knotting all day.'

6 Now, holding the top of the rope in your left hand, grip the rope with your right hand just below the left hand, and proceed to wrap the rope around your left hand. But as you do this you can move the knots along the rope so that when you reach the end of the long rope you can pull off the two knots into your right hand.

7 Quickly reach into your pocket and ditch the two knots, as you say: 'Don't worry. Those knots are knotting. I just need some magic wiffle dust. For this trick it's a must.'

8 Withdraw your hand from your pocket. Now your hand is empty, but pretend you are holding invisible magic dust. Pretend to sprinkle the dust over the ropes. As you do this, unwrap the rope from your left hand. Your audience will be stunned to see that the knots have disappeared completely.

# The professor's nightmare

This is a gem of rope magic. Although first released as a commercial item, it has been around so long and described in so many publications that it is stepping on no toes to include it here. When I was in college I spent a summer in America as a counsellor and magic instructor at a children's summer camp. The camp doctor did this trick with shoelaces to help his young patients cope with the trauma of a doctor's visit. At the other end of the conjuring spectrum Paul Daniels does the very same trick as part of his full evening show – and gets a great reaction from the adults.

Paul Daniels' patter for this is brilliant, a story of three bears, with one rope representing each bear. I have seen other performers using the three lengths of rope as analogies for three political parties before an election, and on one memorable occasion the magician pretended to be a drunken Italian chef trying to make all the pieces of spaghetti match in length. In other words there is much scope for imagination in your patter for this trick.

---

Effect: Three different lengths of rope become the same length.

Require: Three pieces of rope. The long rope should be about as long as the distance between your outstretched arms. The short piece should be about ten inches long (25 cm). The medium piece should be exactly half the length of the long piece plus half the length of the short piece. The correct proportions are vital.

Preparation: None.

Degree of difficulty: ✳✳

## Performance

1 For the purposes of description we will label the ends of the long rope L1 and L2. The ends of the medium rope are M1 and M2. The ends of the short rope are S1 and S2.

2 Tell your audience that you have three pieces of rope, all of different lengths. With your right hand display the short rope, then place one end of it (S1) between your left thumb and forefinger, in the crock of your thumb. Hold it there.

3 Display the medium rope, and place it between your left thumb and forefinger. M1 is now outside S1, and both are held in the left hand, both ropes dangling down.

4 Display the long rope, and place it between your left thumb and forefinger. L1 is now outside M1, which is outside S1. All three ropes are held in your left hand, dangling down.

5 Now take S2, the bottom end of the short rope, and bring it up and around behind the other two ropes, and hold it in your left hand outside L1. Take M2 and bring it up and put it beside S2. Take L2 and bring it up and put it beside M2.

You now have three loops dangling from your left hand. One is small, one medium, and one large. You are holding the six ends in the crock of your thumb, running in this order: S1, M1, L1, S2, M2, L2.

6 Tell your audience that you have three ropes that look uneven, but appearances can be deceptive. If the top ends are even and the bottom ends are even, the ropes must be even.

Saying this, you take L1, M2 and L2 in your right hand. Pulling your hands apart, the ropes stretch until they appear to be even.

7 Now drop the three ends held in your right hand, and you have three even ropes, though you started with three uneven ropes.

8 Take the three dangling ends, and bring them up to your left hand, holding them there. Now pull out S1, and show one rope is short again. Pull out M1 and show one rope medium. Finally, pull out L1 and show the last rope is long again.

9 Toss the ropes out to the audience, to prove that none of the ropes are elastic. You have performed a miracle.

If you follow the instructions here the trick works itself, leaving you free to concentrate on presentation. This is a good one for children and it is a good one for MCs and cabaret work. You can't call yourself a magician until you have mastered the Professor's Nightmare, but luckily it is no nightmare to master.

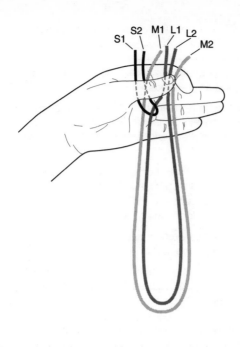

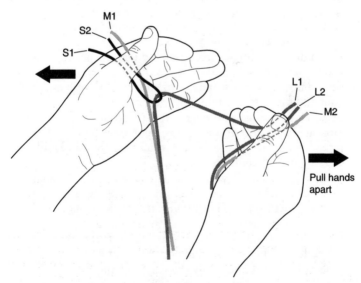

Pull hands apart

**Figure 13** The Professor's Nightmare

# Dissolving knot

This effect is so good it's scary.

> Effect: You tie a knot in a silk headscarf, and the knot slowly unties itself. It's as good as it sounds.
>
> Required: You need a silk headscarf (or a magician's silk handkerchief) that is between 18 inches and 36 inches square. This is not a trick for a pocket handkerchief. You also need six foot of black thread.
>
> Preparation: Tie the thread to one corner of the headscarf. Let's call that corner A. The corner opposite is B. The other end of the thread must be securely attached to the top of the table you are working from. A thumb tack does the trick.
>
> If you are acting as MC for an event, you can attach the other end of the thread to the microphone stand.
>
> Degree of difficulty: ✳✳

## Performance

1  Pick up the headscarf and stand about three feet in front of the table edge where the black thread is attached. Hold corner A in your right hand and allow the headscarf to fall naturally in front of you. The thread should now be hanging at your right side, below your right arm.

2  Reach down with your left hand and take corner B. Twirl the scarf a few times to make a rope of sorts. The black thread should now run across the top of your right thumb and under your right arm to the table top.

3  Bring end A across and over end B (in front of end B as you look at it). As you do this, move your right hand so that the thread is held in position under your right thumb. Hold both ends with your right hand.

4  Letting go of end B with your left hand, reach through the loop formed by the scarf and grab end A (and the thread) with your left fingers. Then pull end A back through the loop.

5  As you slowly draw your hands apart you will form a loose knot in the middle of the scarf. The black thread goes through this knot and should now run over your right thumb.

6  Release corner A and allow the scarf to hang from your right hand (which is holding corner B). If you have done this correctly the thread should run from corner A through the knot, up and over your right thumb, under your right arm, and to the table.

7 Holding the scarf close to your body, you move forward just enough to remove any slack from the thread.

8 If you now extend your right arm, the tension on the thread will cause end A to begin to move upwards. As you continue to move your arm away from the table end A will be drawn up to and completely through the knot. When end A reaches your right hand, grasp end A and let end B go. It will fall downwards. You now are back in the starting position – holding the scarf by end A, with the thread running back to the table.

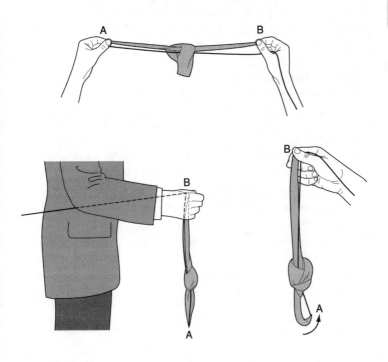

**Figure 14** Dissolving knot

If you want to you are ready to repeat the effect. Normally it is not a good idea to repeat an effect, but this is so spooky you can get away with repeating it once. Not twice. The above routine may sound a bit complicated, but a little practise will show how simple it really is. The key to it is to keep the knot loose. If you pull the knot tight, no amount of magic is going to help you.

# Bill in lemon

The idea of losing a borrowed banknote, then later finding it in the middle of a lemon might sound a bit bizarre, but that is the plot of one of the true classics of cabaret magic. Many great magicians have featured versions of the Bill in Lemon, and the great news is that it is not a difficult trick to master.

Effect: A banknote is put into an envelope, but mysteriously disappears. It is found later in a lemon.

Required: A dozen or so small envelopes, such as wage envelopes. Any small envelope that opens at the side rather then the top will do. You also need three lemons, a bowl, a five pound note, a handwritten IOU for a fiver, which is the same size as the five pound note, a rubber band and a clear plastic bag.

Preparation: First, write the serial number of your five pound note on the back of one of the envelopes, near the bottom. This is envelope A.

Now carefully cut off the gummed flap from another envelope. This is envelope B.

Fold the handwritten IOU and put it in envelope A. Place this envelope on top of the stack of envelopes, so that the serial number is facing up.

Then place envelope B directly on top of envelope A, hiding the serial number from view.

Now square up the envelopes and wrap the rubber band around them to hold them together. Done properly the gummed flap of envelope A will appear to be the flap belonging to envelope B.

The envelopes are now prepared. It's time to prepare the lemon.

On the top of the lemon you will find the spot where the lemon was cut from the tree. With a sharp knife cut carefully around this stem and remove it, but keep it for later.

Now get a thin sharp pencil and push it in through the lemon, making a small cavity in the core of the fruit. Use a very thin pencil so that you don't puncture the juicy portion of the lemon – you want the restored fiver to be dry. A butcher's wooden skewer is even better than a pencil.

Roll the five pound note into a tight roll and push it into the lemon so that it is completely concealed. Use a small dab of glue to replace the stem, so that the lemon looks normal. Now put some small mark on the lemon, so that you can distinguish it from the other two lemons. Maybe nick the skin, or a price label – anything to distinguish it from the other lemons.

Now place the bowl of lemons, the stack of envelopes, a pen, a knife and the small clear plastic bag on the table. You are ready to perform.

Degree of difficulty: ✳✳✳

## Performance

1 Secure a volunteer from the audience and ask him to pick a lemon. Use the Magician's Choice (described in Chapter 03) to force him to pick the lemon with the banknote in it. Put the lemon in the clear plastic bag and tell him to guard it.

2 Borrow a five pound note from your volunteer with the lemon. The way I do this is to ask for a tenner, but settle for a fiver. I then say: 'I asked for a tenner, and you gave me a fiver. So you owe me a fiver. I borrowed a fiver from you, so I owe you a fiver. So let's just call it quits.'

This impeccable piece of warped logic always gets a laugh.

3 Take the borrowed fiver and tell the audience that you will write its serial number on an envelope. Write the serial number on envelope B, at the top of the stack, then fold the note and put it into envelope B.

4 Now here is the clever bit. Take the stack of envelopes in your left hand, and with your right hand take the flap of envelope A and pull it out from the stack, turning the stack over as you do so. To the audience it will look as if you have simply pulled off the top envelope, the one you have put the fiver into. But you have really done something more subtle – you have taken the second envelope out, the one with the IOU.

5 Immediately put the stack of envelopes into your pocket, removing it from the watchful eyes of your suspicious audience. Now take envelope A, with the IOU, and seal down the flap. Hand it to a spectator to hold.

6 Offer a bet to the spectator – if he can tell you the serial number of the five pound note you borrowed from the volunteer with the lemon, he can keep the five pound note. Most spectators will correctly call out the serial number – it is written on the envelope they are holding. If you have chosen a particularly thick spectator, a prompt will get the correct serial number.

7 Turning to the man with the lemon, say: 'You don't mind if he keeps what's in the envelope, do you? After all, you've got a lemon.' Remind him that he chose the lemon before loaning you the five pound note.

8 Turn to the person with the envelope, and tell him to tear it open and remove his winnings. He tears the envelope open, only to find an IOU instead of a five pound note.

9 Turn back to the man with the lemon and hand him a knife, instructing him to cut around the middle of the lemon carefully, then pull the lemon in two. He does this to reveal the hidden five pound note.

10 Take the two halves of the lemon and put them in the plastic bag, disposing of them. This prevents any curious person discovering how the money got into the lemon. Now read the serial number of the note from the back of the torn envelope which contained the IOU, and have the man who cut the lemon confirm that it is indeed the serial number of the five pound note he has in his hand.

You have just accomplished a miracle. As American magician Mark Wilson said, you can make your reputation on this trick alone – so make sure to practise until you get it right.

# Five rules for routining an act

## Rule 1 – Have a strong opening effect

Your opening trick does two things – it grabs people's attention, and it lets them know that they are in the hands of a professional. So make it something simple, direct and strong, and deliver it with confidence. Eating a balloon is a good opener, because it is an unbelievable trick which requires no concentration on the part of the audience. If you do it well the audience will know you are a professional, and will relax and enjoy the show.

## Rule 2 – Involve the audience

While we love watching entertainers, really we are very self-centred creatures. If you involve the audience you draw them into your entertainment, and they will get so much more from it. If they get more, they give more by way of applause.

There are two ways of involving your audience. The first, and easiest, is to pick a person and do a trick on them. The Bill in Lemon effect described earlier is a good example of this type of trick.

The second way of involving the audience is to do something that requires everyone to become part of the trick. In Chapter 09 there is an effect in which everyone is asked to think of a number, and they all come up with 37. That is a perfect effect, if presented by a forceful performer.

## Rule 3 – Use humour

Audiences love a laugh. Even if you are not a natural comedian, several magic tricks almost demand a laugh. Don't be afraid to use them. If you do get a laugh, pause and enjoy it. Don't try to talk over it.

## Rule 4 – Use a formula

A show has a structure. In its simplest form the structure has a beginning, a middle and an end, and this is a good place to start. Have something attention grabbing at the start, something good in the middle, and a strong closing effect. But that structure can be refined. Mix humorous effects with lulls in the entertainment to vary the pace. Throw in dangerous effects or mental effects to keep the audience on the edges of their seats. Experiment with different ways of structuring your show until you get it right.

American children's magician David Ginn recommends a formula for children. He says to begin with something silent (juggling would be perfect) while the children are gathering. Then do something to music. Then do a sucker effect. This is where the magician appears to be getting the trick wrong, but it turns out right in the end. These effects normally pack the laughs. Then follow them with some tricks involving members of your audience. The second from last trick should involve a slight element of danger, and then end on something strong and humorous.

It's not the structure I use, but it has made David Ginn rich, and has a lot to recommend it.

Quentin Reynolds, a top Irish children's magician, suggests a fast-paced opening, then move on to some quieter effects designed to provoke a sense of enchantment and wonder. Then do something with few props, holding the centre stage, then relax with comedy and audience participation, before ending with glamour, noise and colour.

At a lecture for The Magic Circle British comedy magician Geoffrey Durham revealed his formula for a 45-minute cabaret spot. Start with your best trick, followed by a slower effect, possibly but not necessarily involving a member of the audience. Then do a trick with a volunteer, followed by another dip in the energy level with a linking trick not using a volunteer. Then do a strong trick not using a volunteer. Your second last trick should use a volunteer, then end on something flashy.

Personally I like to start quick and flashy, and end strong, using the audience participation tricks in the middle. If I am doing a dangerous trick, such as Russian roulette or escaping from a straitjacket while standing barefoot on broken glass, I end on that, as it is a natural applause cue.

## Rule 5 – End on your strongest effect

This should go without saying. You want your audience to walk away knowing they have seen something special. It is well known that people remember most vividly the opening and the closing of anything, whether it be a lesson in school, a television programme, a newspaper article, or a magic performance. Give them something good to end on, and leave them wanting more. That's the way to get repeat bookings.

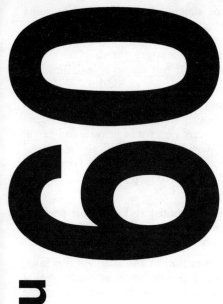

**09**

**mostly mental**

**In this chapter you will learn:**
- How to perform some of the trendiest and hottest effects in magic today
- How to force your entire audience to think of the same number
- How to find out exactly what word someone is thinking
- How to read someone's palm with astonishing realism.

Most magic is trickery. Some sleight of hand is used or some arcane bit of equipment secretly does the work. I don't know about you, but I didn't come into magic to be a glorified practical joker. I was drawn to the mystery, the deep sense that there is more to the world than our five senses reveal, and that something more is mastered by men such as Merlin.

Yes, I had a childish obsession with the warlocks of old, which lead me to read too much about psychic research as a pre-teen and to dream of taming the secret powers of heaven and earth. While my friends saw *Star Wars* and marvelled at the special effects, I read the book and wondered about The Force, that secret power which allowed the Jedi to step beyond the bounds of human ability.

When I was about ten I saw a hypnotist and mentalist perform at a hotel in the Isle of Man. I was convinced he was a genuine psychic, and the show blew my mind.

Several years of meditation, visualisation and self-hypnosis later, I can reveal that there is nothing genuine in it, at least not that I am aware of. But some aspects of magic do come close to the real thing.

Mental magic comes very close to the powers of Merlin. A stage hypnotist can cast spells on his subjects, making them do the most outlandish things. A question and answer performer can summon the spirits to reveal people's innermost thoughts. And a good reader can tell so much about someone it's almost as if he was inside their mind.

That's what magic is about – the genuine magic. Performers such as Derren Brown have made it trendy, but mental magic has always been popular for one reason – we have doubts about how it is done. If you show someone a card trick he may praise your cleverness, but he knows that it is a trick. If you read someone's mind, the disturbing thought remains that there may be something genuine to it.

Today there is an ethical debate within magic. Some performers, such as Uri Geller, claim genuine powers. Others, such as Ian Rowland, claim that they have honed their five senses to give the impression of a sixth. Others operate with the tacit understanding by the audience that they are faking it.

But a word of warning – if you are going to present mental magic, you are better off doing it on its own. Putting in a mental effect in the middle of more conventional magic lets the audience know that you are just using clever means to fool them. Many magicians make the mistake of throwing in the odd mental effect into their act, then wonder why those effects are not doing as well as they hoped they would. If only they knew, that by leaving out the other tricks they would blow their audience away with the mentalism.

Mentalism comes in minor and major varieties. The minor effects are good magic – you pick on someone and read their mind in a very specific way. Telling someone what card they are thinking of is an example. The book test included later in this chapter is one of the best of these minor effects.

The major effects are the ones that involve the whole audience in an emotional way that is totally divorced from magic and props. A stage hypnotist is performing a major effect. A spiritualist medium giving information from the departed to people at random in the audience is performing a major effect. So is a gypsy fortune teller.

In a book such as this there is little scope for exploring the major effects. To learn to be a hypnotist or a medium is a long, hard and very rewarding road. But the first steps in fortune telling are explained. The section on Cold reading is worth the price of the whole book, and then some. Don't neglect it.

Many obsess today with psychics, UFOs, mediums and astrologers but the time is ripe for good mental magicians. Come and dip your toes into the most exciting field in magic.

# Crayon test

Nothing is hotter than psychic powers, and if you can demonstrate these, you will quickly build a reputation as a magician. This is a simple trick that demonstrates eyeless sight – the ability to see without using the known senses. It can be done anywhere. But like all mentalism, showmanship is vital.

---

Effect: Your hands are behind your back. Someone puts a crayon into your hands, and you can identify the colour.

Required: A box of crayons.

Preparation: None.

Degree of difficulty: ✳

---

**Performance**

1 Tell your audience that you have been meditating for a number of years, and have fine tuned your five senses to give the illusion of a sixth sense. You have trained your fingertips to distinguish colours.

2 Give the spectators a box of crayons and ask them to select one secretly. Turn your back on them while they make the selection. Put your hands behind your back and ask them to hand you the crayon.

3 Make a show of running your fingers up and down the crayon, pretending to feel the colour. What you are really doing is scratching the crayon with one nail. Do this just once.

4 Hand the crayon back to the spectator and tell him to put it in the box with the others. While this is being done, bring your hands in front of you. A quick glance at your fingernail will tell you what colour the crayon was. Turn to your spectators and reveal, in a slightly hesitant voice, that you feel you know the colour. The reason you declare this in a hesitant way is that you want to make it appear you are using real senses, not trickery. Too much cockiness and they will know it is a trick. Tell them the colour and take your well-earned applause.

# Predict a finger

Contact mind-reading is as close as a conjurer gets to real magic, with the possible exception of stage hypnosis. You can really read someone's thoughts. Some performers have brought contact mind-reading, also knows as muscle reading, to spectacular heights. American performer George Kreskin used to have a member of the audience hide his cheque somewhere in the theatre, then try to find that cheque merely by walking around holding the hand of the person who had hidden it. He could pick up subtle clues from the hand which led him invariably to his money.

Derren Brown performed a similar stunt on one of his television specials, when he had a street vendor hide a photo of his wife somewhere in a busy London market. Simply by keeping his hands on the man's shoulders Derren was able to locate the photograph.

You may not be able to do quite as much after reading this book, but the effect that follows is a simple version of muscle-reading. It may not work all the time at the start, but with practise you will become startlingly accurate. Explain to your spectator beforehand that you are attempting something more than a conjuring trick. You are using subtle senses, perhaps even a sixth sense, and they have to be as open-minded as you are for the effect to work. That way any failures are seen as proof that you are using hidden powers. It's a win win situation for you.

---

Effect: Your volunteer holds out his hand and concentrates on one finger. You can tell him which of the five fingers he is concentrating on.

Required: A volunteer.

Preparation: None.

Degree of difficulty: *

---

## Performance

1 Ask a volunteer to step forward and hold out his hand, palm down. Ask him to spread his fingers, and to think of one.

2 Emphasising that he is not to give the game away by staring at one finger, ask him to concentrate with his whole being on the finger he is thinking of.

3 With your index finger gently press each one of his outstretched fingers. Four will press down easily. One will resist your push.

4 Holding the finger that resisted your push, tell him that this is the one he was thinking of. Nine times out of ten you will be right. With practise you will be right 99 times out of 100.

# Elephants in Denmark

This is a nice piece of mind-reading that you can do on a single person or a group of people. It will even work on a large audience, over the phone or on the radio. I first saw it described in an editorial in *Boxing Illustrated* by my favourite boxing writer, Bert Randolph Sugar. Why Bert Sugar decided to explain a magic trick in a boxing magazine is beyond me, but like Bert you will have fun with this one.

Effect: You ask someone to think of a number and then do some simple arithmetic to arrive at another, random, number. They convert that number to a letter, think of a country beginning with that letter, then finally think of an animal. You know what country and what animal they arrived at.

Requirements: None.

Preparation: None.

Degree of difficulty: ✳

**Performance**

1 Ask someone (or the entire audience) to pick a number between one and ten that means something to them – their lucky number, the age they first kissed a girl, or any simple number than means something to them.

2 Ask them to multiply this number by nine.

3 If the resulting number has two digits, ask them to add the two digits together. No matter what number they chose, they are now thinking of nine. If they chose one to begin with, one multiplied by nine is nine. If they chose six, then six nines are 54. Five plus four is nine. You get the idea.

4 Ask them to subtract five from their new number. They have to arrive at four – no matter what number they started with. If you tell them they are thinking of four, they will just think you have done a trite mathematical trick. So you don't tell them that.

5 Tell them that each letter in the alphabet corresponds to a number. A is one, B is two, C is three, and so on. Spell this out clearly.

6 Ask them to convert the number they have come up with into its corresponding letter.

7 When they have done this ask them to think of a country beginning with that letter. As they are thinking of D, they are fairly much forced to pick Denmark. (Very few go for Diego Garcia, Djibouti, Dominica, or the Dominican Republic, the only other options.)

8 Now ask them to spell their country in their head. Ask them to select the second letter of the country (E) and ask them to think of an animal beginning with that letter. Again this is a psychological force – most people will go for an elephant.

9 Pretend to be reading their mind – stare deeply at them, look thoughtful and mysterious, then tell them that they must be

in a zoo – that's the only place you'd find an elephant in Denmark. Watch the amazement on their faces.

This is a beautiful effect if done seriously. Play it up – act the part of a psychic. And if you do it on a number of people at the same time, it can look like you have some mysterious hold over their minds. But whatever you do, do not repeat this trick.

# Five rules of mentalism

## Rule 1 – Decide on who you are

Are you a magician doing some puzzling mental effects? Or are you pretending to have real powers? For most magicians the answer falls somewhere in between. They make the claim that they have no powers beyond the ordinary; what they have done is to fine tune their five senses to create the illusion of a sixth sense. Audiences today seem to accept this. It allows them to believe that we have a vast well of unused brain potential, without asking them to believe in the supernatural. Initially this is probably the best approach to take. But be consistent. Don't claim supernatural powers for one effect and fine-tuned senses for another. The audience will not accept that.

The other thing you have to decide is whether to mix mentalism with magic, or do both separately. I believe that you will achieve the best results if you present the mental effects separately from your magic. You are quite welcome to disagree – but at least be consistent.

## Rule 2 – This is not a joke

When you are doing mental magic you are playing with people's belief systems. While you may not claim supernatural powers, you are pushing the boundaries. So treat the audience with the respect that they deserve. If you present mentalism in a serious way, you will achieve far more than if you try the Tommy Cooper approach.

This doesn't mean that you have to leave your sense of humour in the parking lot. Some effects lend themselves to gentle humour, which will always go down well. You can even throw in joke items such as the No Gag and the Baby Gag, described in the previous chapter. Just leave the clowning aside.

## Rule 3 – Respect your volunteers

No area of magic depends so much on volunteers as mentalism. You can't read minds if people won't allow you to read their minds. If you embarrass your volunteers then your audience will cringe. If they cringe, they will not applaud. So treat everyone who assists you with respect. When their role is finished, be gracious and lead the applause for them.

I use a light, comedy approach to mentalism, often poking fun at my assistants. But I never belittle them. It is all in fun, and no disrespect is intended. And I always thank them sincerely. If you can fake sincerity, you have it made.

## Rule 4 – Be smooth

There have been many skilled hypnotists in Britain. None achieved the success of Paul McKenna. His secret? He had been a DJ on *Capital Radio*. When he switched to stage hypnosis his voice and presentation were so much smoother and more professional than his rivals.

Don't fumble your patter. Decide what you are going to say with each effect, and rehearse it until the patter is as smooth as the moves. Remember that a trick is not just the secret, it is the presentation.

## Rule 5 – Be wrong

That goes against the grain, but you are doing mental magic, not balancing accounts. It's all right to be wrong. In fact, it can add to the illusion. If you ask someone to concentrate on the serial number of a five pound note, then flawlessly reel off the number, your audience will know something is not kosher. But if you hesitate slightly, start revealing numbers, then get one wrong, then get back on track, the illusion that you are reading a mind is perfect.

Often at a circus the high wire act will fake a fall, then perform a stunningly difficult manoeuvre. The fake fall heightens the tension, and makes the final success all the sweeter. Follow their lead, but don't overdo it.

# The book test

This is a classic. The plot is simplicity itself. Invite an audience member to open a book at random and look at a word. You tell them what word they are looking at.

There are dozens of ways of doing a book test. Some are simple. Some are elaborate and involve extensive memory work. Some involve specially printed books that can pass for real books, but which have been subtly gaffed. Some use one book, some two, some as many as half a dozen.

After looking at a number of these methods I am still happy with the version I have been doing for a number of years. It is simple, it can be done with any two books you are presented with, and it can be done without any advance preparation work.

---

Required: At least two books of roughly similar length. I often have half a dozen books, and that allows me great scope for comedy as my volunteer picks the book they want from my choice. I make sure the books are all very different. Asking a person to choose between six Agatha Christies is not my idea of an entertaining book test.

But you could just as easily do this casually in a library or bookshop, by taking down any two titles and giving them to your spectator.

Preparation: None.

Degree of difficulty: ✳✳

---

## Performance

1 Ask your spectator to choose a book. Milk this for comedy if it is appropriate. Don't bother if the setting is wrong.
2 When the spectator has picked a book, and satisfied himself that all the books are genuine, take his book from him and flick to the end, remarking that there are roughly so many words in the book. Let's say that the book is roughly 360 pages long.
3 While you are flicking to the end of the book you need to stop somewhere in the middle and glimpse the first word on that page. Let's say you stop briefly on page 197, and the word you spot is lemon. Remember the word and the page number.

With a little bit of practise you will become very good at spotting a word and page number, and quickly you won't even need to stop as you riffle through the pages to find the end.

4 Hand the book back to the spectator, telling him that you are going to pick a number between one and 360 at random. Pick up one of the other books and hold it with your right hand. With your left thumb begin to riffle through the pages at one corner, telling your volunteer to shout stop at any point he likes.

5 It is very easy to make sure that you have riffled roughly into the middle of the book by the time he shouts stop. Immediately open the book and look at the page number. It doesn't matter what that is, because you are going to tell him that it is page 197. Close the book immediately so that he doesn't realise you are conning him.

6 Continue in your psychic mode: 'You stopped me at page 197. So could you turn to page 197 of your book? I want you to concentrate on the first word of that page. See it clearly in your head. I'm beginning to pick up something. It's a short word? An object of some sort? For some reason I taste something tart in my mouth. Is the word lemon?'

Take your applause. You have done the impossible.

## Magician wins

This is a top class mental mystery that can become a big item in a stage show. I recently saw top telly magician Keith Barry do this with the help of pop star Samantha Mumba. Samantha picked out four boxes, leaving Keith with one. She got four teddy bears, while he was left with a poisonous scorpion.

There are as many variations on this trick as there are magicians performing it. I like the one that follows because it is simple, it looks very good, and there are no scorpions involved.

All you need is five envelopes and a banknote. The higher the denomination of the banknote the better. Another idea is to put your fee for the show into an envelope. Whenever I do this I write a cheque for an outrageous amount – no point in letting the audience know you work for the same fee as everyone else.

Put a small pencil mark on the corner of one envelope. Make sure the mark is discrete, but easy for you to see. This is the envelope that the banknote or cheque goes into. When I perform this on stage for adults I always make sure to put a lottery ticket in the other four envelopes. The reason for this is simple. If the audience volunteers open their envelopes and find nothing, while you win the money, you can appear to be a smug know-it-all. But if they get something it makes them feel better, and makes you look better.

If you are doing this on stage you are probably getting paid for it or it is a charity event, so paying out four pounds will not hurt you.

> Effect: A banknote is put into one of five envelopes. The envelopes are well shuffled, and four volunteers each pick an envelope. They have chosen the empty ones, leaving the magician holding the prize.
>
> Required: A banknote. Five envelopes, one of which is marked with a small pencil dot on two of the corners, so that you can identify it instantly.
>
> Preparation: None, except marking one of the envelopes so that you can identify it quickly.

## Performance

1 Begin the trick with five envelopes. The banknote is in the marked envelope. The others are empty, or contain lottery tickets. If you are working on a stage invite four volunteers up. Give one of them the bundle of envelopes and tell them to shuffle them thoroughly. If you are working in a more intimate setting, hand the five envelopes to someone and ask them to shuffle them.

2 When you take the envelopes back casually spread them and spot where the marked envelope is. Cut the stack of envelopes, so that the envelope with the banknote is second from the top.

3 Hand the stack of envelopes to one of your four volunteers and tell him to spell the word magic, transferring one envelope from the top to the bottom of the pile as he calls out each letter. He is to keep the envelope that falls on the letter C.

4 Now take the stack of four envelopes and hand it to the next spectator, telling him to spell out the word magic, transferring one envelope from the top to the bottom of the pile as he calls out each letter. He too is to keep the envelope that falls on the letter C.

5 Go through the same procedure with the third and fourth volunteer, telling them to keep the envelope that falls on the letter C.

6 The fourth spectator hands you the final envelope. For a laugh, you spell the word magic and hold up the final envelope.

7 Now get each one of your volunteers to open their envelope. As they do, revealing that they are not the winner, lead the applause for them and let them leave the stage. Finally you are alone, and you open the final envelope to reveal that you are the winner.

# The masks of death

There is a popular effect sold for next to nothing by joke shops and magic shops. There are three cards in an envelope and the spectator is asked to choose one. The performer reveals that he knew the selection. The problem with this is that if you were a real mentalist, you wouldn't need to limit the selection to three cards. So there has to be a reason for limiting the selection to three, and also there has to be some hook to add fascination to the effect. I found small brass masks in a pound shop one day and came up with this routine. This falls into the category of bizarre magic. Bizarre magic is a small genre in which the tricks all have an occult slant, and the storytelling is as important as the magic. That is why I have gone into more detail than usual on the patter.

Effect: The performer takes out of a box three brass masks enamelled with different colours. He explains that primitive people believed that wearing masks allowed one to assume the identity of a god. He asks the spectator to shuffle the masks then select one. When the mask is selected, the performer looks at it, then gives the spectator a very accurate personality reading, before revealing that he knew in advance which mask the spectator would be drawn to. This is a charming close-up effect, and because of its fortune telling aspect it will appeal to women.

Required: A box and three small masks – you can make them out of card if you can't find suitable small masks in a knick-knack shop.

Preparation: Let us say that one mask is black, one is gold and one is red. Put a sticker on the back of the black mask, but not on the others. On the base of the box write *you will choose the gold mask*. Inside the box put your business card, with *you will choose the red mask* written on the back of it. Place all three masks in the box.

## Performance (patter indented)

1  Today we are a sophisticated society and we do not believe in such things, but for thousands of years man believed that gods controlled our destiny. There were gods of rain, gods of thunder, gods of sunshine and good harvests. If you offended a god, then watch out. But if you placated the gods, then things would go well for you and your tribe. This belief was called Shamanism, and is still common in parts of Africa, Asia, and South America. Each tribe had a special person, the shaman or witch doctor, whose job it was to communicate with the gods. They would go into a trance and assume the identity of the god they wished to placate. And the best way to assume the identity of the god was to wear the mask that represented that god.

2  I have a number of small masks here (take the three masks from the box) and I would like you to just move them around the table like this, any way you wish.

   Allow a spectator to move the masks around the table (but not to lift them from the table or turn them over). When she is satisfied, continue.

3  Now put your finger on one of the masks (spectator does so). You've picked an interesting mask. In fact, your choice tells me something about your character. Do you mind?

4  Now deliver a reading based on the Cold reading, described later in this chapter. You don't have to deliver the full reading – a third of it will be enough in most cases. End the reading on this line:

   In fact, knowing your character as I do, there was only one mask you could have chosen.

5  Then reveal that you knew the selection in advance. If the spectator has their finger in the black mask, turn the other two over, then ask them to turn the black over. They will see that it is the only one marked on the back with a sticker. If they chose gold, tell them to turn over the box, where their choice is revealed. If they chose red, tell them to take your business card out of the box and read the back.

   Because it includes a character reading this is a stronger effect than you would imagine, but obviously you do not repeat it.

# The centre tear

This is one of the best tricks you will learn. Do it well and you will get a reputation as someone with remarkable powers – it is so good it borders on real magic.

---

Effect: Someone writes a name on a piece of paper, which is torn up and dumped or burnt. You stare into their eyes, then correctly read their minds to reveal the name they were thinking of.

Required: A square of paper, roughly two to three inches (8cm) square. A biro.

Preparation: None.

Degree of difficulty: ✳✳

---

## Performance

1  Show the blank sheet of paper to your volunteer and explain that you are going to try and read their mind, but you need them to focus their thoughts. That is why you have the blank piece of paper.

2  Draw a small television screen in the dead centre of the square of paper, with the screen a little over an inch (3 cm) across. Tell the volunteer that you want them to focus on a film or television personality, alive or dead. Imagine them on the small screen.

3  To help them focus, hand them a biro and ask them to write the name of the star on the TV screen. Tell them that they will focus better if they print the name in good clear handwriting.

4  Ask them to concentrate on the name, then fold the paper in half. Ask them to fold the paper in half a second time. They are now holding a small square of folded paper.

5  Take this piece of paper from the volunteer and tear it down the middle. Now tear both halves across their middle. You now have a number of bits of paper, but if you look carefully it should be obvious that one of the pieces is the centre piece, which contains the screen of the television. This centre piece will be easy to spot.

6  Now shuffle the bits of paper around in your hands until the centre piece is on top. Transfer the pieces into your left hand, but keep the centre piece concealed in your right hand as you reach into your pocket for a lighter or box of matches.

7  Holding the pieces in your left hand, set fire to them and drop them into an ashtray.

8  While the pieces are burning you can bring your hands up and cover your face while you mime concentration. Under cover of this use your thumb to open the folded piece you have retained in your right hand. A little practise will show how easy it is to read this now.

   Alternatively you can turn from your volunteer to put away the matches or lighter, reading the centre piece as you do so.

9  As you both look at the burning pieces, say that you are beginning to pick up some impressions. Of course, you know exactly who they are thinking about, because you have read the name they wrote. Talk in vague terms for a moment – a male figure, beginning to go grey at the temples, etc. – then become more specific as you hone in on their thoughts.

10  Finally reveal the name of their chosen personality.

Of course, the centre tear is far more versatile than just finding out their favourite personality. Any thing they think of – a name, a number, a place, a favourite food – can be 'mind-read' using this powerful technique.

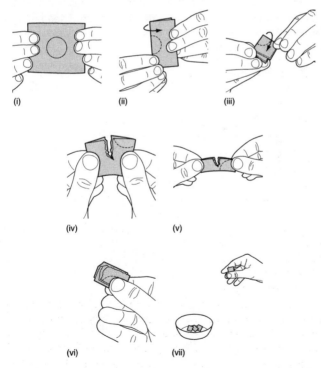

(i)  (ii)  (iii)

(iv)  (v)

(vi)  (vii)

**Figure 15** Centre tear

# Predict a number

Imagine asking your audience to think of any number, and you can tell them the number the majority of them have come up with. How? Perhaps you have influenced their thoughts through mental telepathy. They will certainly believe that after this trick. It is unusual in that it is not guaranteed to work. It is what magicians call a psychological force. You use subtle language to guide their thoughts along the right path. Like muscle-reading, described earlier, it can let you down. But when it goes right, as it generally does, it is very powerful, because there is no trickery. It is genuine.

> Effect: You ask your entire audience to think of a number between one and a hundred. Most of them arrive at the same number – the number you predicted beforehand. You repeat the trick, and the result is the same. Of course, this trick can just as easily be done one-on-one.
>
> Required: A notebook with two predictions in it.
>
> Preparation: In the notebook write the number 35. Then put an X through the five and write 7 after it, so it looks like you wrote 35, then changed your mind to 37.
>
> On the next page write 68. You could just as easily write your predictions on a flip-chart, or put them in an envelope in your pocket.
>
> Degree of difficulty: ✱✱

## Performance

1 Tell your audience that it is possible for one mind to tune into another, through mental telepathy, but both sides have to be willing to be open to the process so you will begin with something simple. You want everyone to make their minds blank.

2 If you want a laugh at this point, turn to someone in the front row, look at him, then look at the audience, saying: 'It didn't take him long, did it?'

3 Now ask everyone to imagine a vegetable. Immediately announce that the vegetable you were thinking of was a carrot. Most people, under pressure, will have thought of a carrot, so well over half the audience may feel you have begun to make a mental connection.

4 Continue: 'Now we are going to try something more difficult.' From here on the presentation is vital, and you must get it right. The wording is strategically designed to force a particular number on your spectators.

5 'I am thinking of a number, and I am going to try to transmit it to you, so make your minds blank.'

6 'The number I am thinking of is an odd number.'

7 'It has two digits.'

8 'And they are different from each other. In other words I am not thinking of 33, 44, 55, or any number where the digits repeat.'

9 'Are you ready? I am thinking of a two-digit number, and it is odd. The number is between …'

10 Pause. Psychologically you have just set a limit on the number, but the audience doesn't know what that limit is. Their minds go blank, which is what you want.

11 'The number is between ten and 50. Please think of the first number that comes into your head.'

12 'Have you got the number? Hold that thought.'

13 Go to your notebook or flipchart and show it. Announce that you were thinking of 37. The vast majority of the audience will be thinking of 37 as well. A ripple of astonishment will pass through the crowd. You then remark that you were going to transmit 35, but changed your mind at the last minute. The few who are thinking of 35 are now convinced.

14 Announce that you are going to repeat the experiment. 'Let's try a second number. Make your mind blank. This one is an even number, it has two digits, and both are different.'

15 'Are you ready? A two-digit number, it's even, and it's between …'

16 Pause again.

17 'It's between 50 and a hundred. Think of the first number that comes into your head, and hold it there.'

18 Turn back to your prediction and reveal 68. Your audience will be stunned, because the vast majority are thinking of 68. This is called a psychological force, and is a very strong piece of magic, which was popularised by Argentinean magician Tony Slydini. Try it and you will be amazed at the audience response.

# Cold reading – the secret of fortune telling

I first came across the classic reading in Lee Earle's *The Gentle Art of Cold Reading*, a gem of a book and tape which I would highly recommend. The classic reading is 12 statements that manage to sound specific while being very vague. American psychology researchers came up with the 12 statements in the 1950s after studying too many horoscopes and scoffing too many fortune cookies.

The beauty of the 12 statements is that most people will feel that the statements apply to themselves and their character. If you give someone a valid reason for accepting the statements (ie, tell them that you are reading their palms) then 85 to 90 per cent of people will believe that you are giving them an accurate character reading. They will also believe that the character reading is fairly detailed and specific.

I have rewritten the 12 statements into a script suitable for palm reading. The script gives a bit of waffle beforehand to add to the credibility of the reading, and gives an upbeat ending. The script is 400 words long, and will take about two and a half minutes to deliver. In other words, it won't kill you to learn it. The best way to learn something like this was explained to me by an actor. He said that to memorise a speech, read it out loud five times in a row, for five days in a row. That will take you a little over ten minutes a day for less than a week. After that it is fairly much burned into your memory.

This is just the beginning of character reading, or fortune telling. Most professional readers use a tool such as tarot cards, and they observe their clients carefully, searching for clues. If you have the empathy for it and put the time in, you will find all that falling into place naturally. But there is nothing wrong with sticking to the basic script. It packs a punch.

---

Effect: You hold someone's palm, stare at it for a few moments, then deliver a startlingly accurate personality reading for that person.

Required: A good memory.

Preparation: Memorise the script.

Degree of difficulty: ✳✳✳ (unless you have a photographic memory)

## Performance (patter indented)

1 Ask your volunteer to step forward, smile at them to build up empathy, then begin to deliver the following script.

Are you left handed or right handed? Right handed ... Could I have a look at your left hand, please? Just hold it out in front of you. (Take her hand gently in yours at this point.)

2 Both hands tell us different things about a person. The left hand tells us about your basic character. It's your non-dominant hand, and it's governed by your subconscious. The right hand is governed by the conscious mind, and is less useful to us. Leaving aside the various lines, the life-line and so on, we can tell a great deal just by the way you hold your hand, the shape of your hand, your fingers, whether you hold them apart or together. That's what I'm going to concentrate on right now. I am going to try and tell you some basic things about your character just from the way you have presented your hand to me.

3 The first thing that I can see is that you have a strong need to be liked by others, and for them to admire you. You have a tendency to be critical of yourself. I see that you have a great deal of unused capacity which you have not yet put to use.

4 While I can see some personality weaknesses, you are generally able to compensate for them. Your love life has been a bit topsy-turvy at times. Your hand shows me that while you like to appear disciplined and controlled on the outside, you tend to be worrisome and insecure on the inside. This leads you to have serious doubts as to whether you have made the right decision or done the right thing.

5 Variety is the spice of life, and you require a certain amount of change and variety, otherwise you can become dissatisfied and feel hemmed in. You pride yourself on being an independent thinker, and don't accept the opinions of others unless they can back them up. Experience has taught you that it is unwise to be too frank in revealing yourself to others.

6 You are an enigma – at times you are extroverted, affable, sociable, while at other times you are introverted, wary, reserved. Some of your aspirations tend to be a little unrealistic. However, on the whole your hand reveals depths of character which will stand you in good stead.

7 I don't know if your realise it or not, but you have some psychic ability, and at some point in the future you may wish to develop that intuitive gift. Thank you for allowing me to look at your palm, the roadmap of your soul. I hope you got something useful out of what I had to say.

8 Gently let go the person's hand, and smile at them. The reading is over.

There you have it in a nutshell. If you are doing this for a number of people you can just deliver the same reading time after time, as long as they don't overhear one another. They won't remember the details clearly enough to realise they are all hearing the same spiel. If people are able to overhear each other's readings, just deliver the opening remarks as usual, then begin the meat of the reading – the 12 statements – in the middle rather than at the beginning. So vary the order of the steps in the above reading. When you come to the closing statement, just change it slightly. Instead of telling them they have psychic ability, tell them they have a natural empathy with people that might express itself as a healing ability. That will be enough to make it sound like a completely fresh reading.

There you have the secret of being a psychic without being the seventh son of a seventh son. Guard this secret closely, and use it often.

# Five rules of marketing yourself

## Rule 1 – Take out a classified ad

Look in the Classified Ads section of your local papers, and see where the entertainers have their ads. In some areas they advertise in every paper, while in other areas one paper gets all the business. Don't try to be clever by going for the paper the others are ignoring – they probably have a good reason for not advertising there.

Don't undersell yourself, and don't be vague. Magician available is not enough. If you are going for the adult close-up market, say so: Sophisticated magician available for your function. Corporate enquiries welcome. If you want to specialise in children's magic, be equally specific: Children love Kermit the Konjurer. Phone the fun line now.

Although it sounds smarmy, don't leave out the words 'Children love ...' That's what gets the phone ringing.

If you want to keep your options open, then put in two separate ads, one for children's work and one for other work.

Regularity is important. If you decide to have a classified ad, then have it every week. It looks more professional than a hit and miss approach, and most papers will do a good deal if you block-book a few months of ads. The first gig you get pays for them all, so splash out.

## Rule 2 – Contact your local promoters

If you check in your Yellow Pages or other telephone directory you will find a list of local entertainment agencies and promoters. Most will have a magician or two that they use regularly, but if they have your details they will keep you in mind.

Phone them all and introduce yourself, then send on a resume of what you can offer them. After this leave them alone. Pester power does not work with promoters.

A promoter once told me that there are two ways to succeed in showbiz. Get a good manager, which is difficult, or have your details with 50 promoters. If you get just a handful of gigs from each every year, you will be rushed off your feet.

## Rule 3 – Contact your local hotels

Hotels, like promoters, have their own list of entertainers. But unlike promoters they rarely display loyalty to those entertainers. Contact each hotel in your region, speak to the banqueting manager, and send her your details. If you contact enough people, you will be surprised at the results.

## Rule 4 – Visit the hairdresser

This invaluable bit of advice will double the income of any children's entertainer. Produce an attractive flier (it can be black and white, which keeps costs down) and ask a number of hairdressers in your locality to display a pile of them. Most will be happy to do so. Present them with a nice bouquet of balloon flowers, and you will rarely be refused.

Even in this politically correct age birthday parties are still organised by mums. Mums get their hair done regularly, and if they pick up your flier, you will get the business.

## Rule 5 – Pass around your card

Business cards are easy to get. Every shopping centre has the print-your-own-card machines, or you could spend a few quid and get a professional card. Keep it simple – your performing name, an indication of what you do and your contact details. Once you get the cards don't leave them on the dresser at home. Give them out to your friends, to work colleagues, to anyone who seems even half-way interested in the fact you are a magician. Or just leave piles of them discretely in public places such as hotels and pubs.

But above all, keep a supply in your pocket. If someone says they are looking for a magician for an event, it looks professional if you can just whip out a card and present it to them. Remember the Boy Scouts' motto – be prepared.

If you follow the five rules of marketing you can quickly build up a profitable sideline, or even a new career, in magic. Then make sure your show lives up to your publicity. If your show is good enough the sixth (and most important) rule of marketing kicks in; there is nothing quite as effective as word-of-mouth recommendations.

# 10

## children's magic

In this chapter you will learn:
- How children are different from adults when it comes to entertaining
- The importance of storytelling and strong presentation
- How to stretch a balloon to fifteen minutes of entertainment
- The secret behind the Chinese linking rings.

I was walking along the road in my car, with a tiger under one of my arms with one eye called Fred. I don't know what his other eye was called. Suddenly the ship struck a rock and began to sink, so I had to swim for the shore. I nearly drowned. I wouldn't have made it except I had a parachute. When I got to the house I knocked at the door. A man opened the door in his pyjamas. I thought that's a strange place to have a door, in your pyjamas. But I said nothing. I cycled past him and sat down in front of the fridge to write this article on how to keep children entertained …

They say that you can divide the world into two types of people – those who divide the world into two types of people, and those who don't. If that is true, then you can divide children's entertainers into two types – those who like children, and those who don't.

Some magicians make a proud boast of not liking children. The children are little monsters who have to be worked around to get the fat fee at the other end of the hour. These crusty conjurers tell stories about how they got the better of the children – about how they pinch the little dears when their parents are out of the room, and how they 'accidentally' tread on the toes of hecklers. Sadly this is not a joke. There are performers who overcome their antipathy towards children because the birthday party market is the biggest and most lucrative market available to most magicians. Those people are a disgrace to our profession.

If you do not like children, stop right here and move on to the next chapter.

But if you do like children – or even if you are a neutral, willing to approach them with an open mind and heart – then there are few branches of magic more rewarding. And I don't mean financially, though that side adds up pretty well too. You know that what you are doing is working when you see the look of wonder on a child's face, or when you hear the beautiful sound of a room full of kids laughing with you.

The American magician Lee Earle had some useful words of advice for children's magicians. He points out that the child you are performing for may not have been lucky enough to have seen a live magician before you. You could well be the first live performer that child sees, and that is a powerful and privileged position to be in. Lee Earle says that you should always strive to be the best magician that child has ever seen. That way the child grows up inspired, and with a love of live entertainment. If you are a cheap imitation of a children's entertainer, the child will have a more cynical attitude towards you and the art you represent.

Those are wise words, and whenever I am feeling cheesed off or lethargic as I step from my car and hear the noises of the party ahead of me, I try to remember. The children are young and innocent. They deserve our best.

Entertaining children is different from entertaining adults, because children are different. If you get on their wavelength, they will love you. But they are not push-overs. If you execute your tricks clumsily, they will see through you. And they will take great delight in bursting your bubble.

On the other hand, children have an open mind, and you can make them believe – truly believe – in the magic.

# Five rules for entertaining children

## Rule 1 – Children love colour and spectacle

Why are cartoons the most popular form of entertainment for under-tens? Because they are bright, colourful and simple. Make your magic bright, colourful and simple. If you are using props (and children love props) make sure they are brightly painted. Don't be afraid of the traditional trappings – the wand and the hat. Many of the tricks described in this book using a biro or pencil can just as easily be done with a wand for children. And conversely, any trick using a wand can be done with a biro for adults.

## Rule 2 – Don't talk down to them

Growing up I had uncles who came into the house and asked how I was doing at school. I had one uncle who swept into the house, swung me upside down by the ankles, and tickled me until I went purple. You know who my favourite was.

If you want to entertain children, then you have to get on their wavelength. Obviously in the current climate tickling is completely out, but so too should be the patronising questions about how they are doing at school. Talk to them about something they are interested in, and don't talk down to them.

# Rule 3 – Use stories in your patter

Children love stories. If you can create a story around a piece of magic, then you will hold their attention all the better. Don't be afraid of repetition in a story. You can get the children really into it by using this technique.

An example from my show is the following verbal lead-in to a trick. I got this tip from an old magician Ken Little, and modified it to suit my style.

'Boys and girls, it was the night before Christmas and all through the house not a creature was stirring, not even a ... (pause) ... hippopotamus. I was stretched out by the fire when who should call?'

Children – Santa Claus.

'That's right. I recognised his blue coat.'

Children – He has a red coat.

'Sorry, his red coat. And he had a beautiful black beard.'

Children – A white beard.

'Sorry, a white beard. And he arrived on a bicycle.'

Children – In a sleigh.

'Sorry. A sleigh. And it was towed by eight tiny hedgehogs.'

Children – Reindeers.

'Sorry – reindeers. And one of them had a silly name. Humphrey, I think.'

Children – Rudolf.

'Sorry, of course it was Rudolf. I remember now. There was a song about him. Rudolf the green-nosed reindeer had a very snotty nose, and if you ever saw it you would even say blow your nose Rudolf, you look disgusting.'

Children – It was a red nose.

And so on. Eventually this will lead to the introduction of my next prop.

The above might sound silly, but children will respond, and their shouts get louder and louder as you go along. They love stories and they love repetition.

In my show I have a cast of characters I chat about – friends of mine that the children never meet. The two most popular are Zebediah Snotnose and Johnny Pinkistews, who is always annoyed because people get his name wrong and call him Johnny Stinky-poohs.

If you are stuck for stories, pick up any book of children's fairy tales. My favourite collections are the *Grimm Tales*, and James Jacobs' *Celtic fairy-tales*.

## Rule 4 – Be rude

Rude is good for children. If a child who is helping you makes a mistake call him a silly sausage. Make a farting noise and blame a child. Ways of tapping into children's love of rebellion include using the odd rude word – rude, but not vulgar. Fart is fine, but the other f-word is an absolute non-starter. Children love any mention of bums, snot, even pooh (but not s**t). If you grab a child's foot in the middle of your performance, pull off his shoe, smell his sock and pull a face; you will get a great reaction.

Calling children names is perfectly acceptable, as long as the names are ludicrous. I call children banana-heads and silly sausages all the time. Those names are so silly that no offence is intended, or taken. But never call a child anything that might even remotely be hurtful. Never make fun of their appearance or of what they are wearing. And never mimic them.

## Rule 5 – Children love anarchy

If you look in the window of any classroom when the teacher steps outside, you will know that children are the original rebels without cause or clue. They love running riot. They have so much physical energy to burn off, and so few inhibitions. If you can capture that in your show, making your show the wildest hour in town, then you are on to a winner. But you must stay in control.

Children also love the ridiculous. Asking a question that is completely off the wall works well. When a boy is wearing his school uniform and his tie, I often ask if he is a bank manager, as only bank managers wear ties these days. When a young girl is up helping me, I often ask her if she is married.

Bear the above rules in mind and you are ready to leave behind your inhibitions and begin entertaining children. The first few effects are simple. Later in the chapter we will cover whole routines that you can drop straight into an act. They will take work, but they are worth the effort.

# The rising wand

This is a trick that is very suitable for a younger audience, though I saw the late Tommy Cooper do a very funny version with the wand replaced by a fork. Use your imagination and you might come up with your own variation.

---

Effect: You put your wand into a bottle. Immediately it begins to rise up out of the bottle. Eventually it tumbles right out of the bottle.

Required: One bottle. One wand. Two feet of thin fishing line or thin black thread. The wand can be made quite easily. Get an 18-inch length of quarter or half inch wooden doweling rod from a DIY shop, and paint it black. Paint the last inch on both sides white. You have a wand.

Preparation: Glue the fishing line to the bottom of the wand with a dab of superglue. Tie the other end of the line to your jacket button.

Degree of difficulty: *

---

## Performance

1 Take the wand and put it inside the bottle, with the end with the line attached at the bottom.
2 Move slightly back from the wand and bottle. As you do the line between the wand and your jacket button will tighten.
3 It is a simple matter to move back an inch or two – even to just lean back – and the wand will be pulled up out of the bottle by the thread.
4 Moving just slightly you can cause the wand to jump a little a few times. Finally back away slowly and the wand will rise up and fall from the bottle.

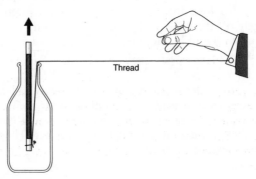

Thread

**Figure 16** Rising wand

# The magic knitting needles

This is an old effect that I came across in *Sleight of Hand, A Practical Manual of Legerdemain for Amateurs & Others,* by Edwin Sachs, first published in 1885. A wise man once said that for every book, video or DVD you buy that is up to date, buy two that come from before 1950. A trick that hasn't been seen in 60 years is as new to an audience as a freshly-created effect.

Obviously it is not easy to get your hands on DVDs and videos from before 1950, but there are plenty of books out there, and some are gems.

I altered the presentation of this effect and made it into a nice routine for children.

---

Required: Twelve brass rings, such as curtain or shower rings. Tie six together with bits of wool, and leave six loose. One magic wand. An 18-inch wooden dowel painted black, with white tips, is perfect. One colourful headscarf. Two knitting needles.

Preparation: Leave your wand in your suitcase, or hidden behind something on your table. Have the six tied together rings already on the wand, near one end. Have the six loose rings in a pocket or on your table.

Degree of difficulty: *

---

## Performance

1 Call for a volunteer to help you do the magic. As your volunteer comes forward take the wand in your left hand. This hand conceals the six rings on the wand. Take the six loose rings and ask the volunteer to put the rings, one at a time, onto the end of the wand.

    You now have a wand with 12 rings on it. Six are tied together, and are hidden under your left hand. Six are loose.

2 Tell your audience that this trick is best done under cover of darkness. Drape a headscarf over the wand and over your left hand. The loose rings are covered by the headscarf.

3 Put your right hand on the other end of the wand, under the headscarf. Now for the magic. Tilt the wand so that the six loose rings slide towards your right hand. Allow them to slide under your right hand, so that they are concealed there. At the same time allow the six tied rings under your left hand to slide free, ending up in the middle of the wand, hidden by the headscarf.

4 Take away your left hand. To the audience you have just transferred the wand from one hand to another, but under cover of the headscarf you have really switched the two sets of rings. The magic is now done. The rest is presentation.

5 Tell your volunteer to feel under the headscarf to confirm that the rings are still there. She will confirm this. Don't worry – she won't feel the woollen knots between the rings. She will believe that she is feeling the six loose rings she put on the wand a moment earlier.

6 Now tell your volunteer to pick up the two knitting needles and begin to mime knitting above the headscarf. Suggest that she imagine she has wool. Suggest the colour of the wool – the same colour as you used to tie the rings, of course.

7 As she does this, tell the children that your mother taught you a rhyme to remember how to knit. It goes like this: In through the bunny hole, around the big tree. Out through the bunny hole, and off goes she. Get the children to chant along with you.

8 As they say 'Off goes she!' you whip away the headscarf with your left hand, revealing the six rings. With your left hand lift the rings off the wand and display them all tied together with wool the same colour as your volunteer imagined she was knitting with.

This is a simple trick that requires little skill and not a great deal of preparation – yet it always goes down well with a young audience.

# The self-inflating balloon

This can be done for children or done to music as part of a colourful cabaret act.

Effect: A bag is turned over and a balloon falls out. You let the air out of the balloon then put it back in the bag. When the bag is turned over the balloon falls out fully inflated again.

Required: A large paper bag, one of the type that folds open for groceries. Two identical small balloons. Some double-sided sticky tape.

Preparation: Inflate both balloons, but keep them small enough that both will fit into the bag easily. Using a small piece of double-sided tape, gently attach one balloon to the base of the bag. Put the other balloon in on top.

Degree of difficulty: *

**Performance**

1 Hold up the paper bag, then turn it upside down. One of the small balloons will tumble out.

2 Pick up the balloon and untie the knot, releasing the air. Display the deflated balloon.

3 Reach into the bag and gently pull the second balloon free of the sticky tape, while attaching the uninflated balloon to the tape. To the audience it should appear that you have only put an uninflated balloon into the paper bag.

4 Step back, take a deep breath, and blow towards the bag. This is the time to remember all those old Charlie Chaplin and Buster Keaton movies. Really exaggerate and mime the blowing, so that the audience are in no doubt what you are doing.

5 Step up to the bag, take it in your hands, and turn it upside down. The inflated balloon will fall out of it.

6 Crumple up the bag and toss it away, getting rid of the uninflated balloon at the same time.

# More thoughts on entertaining children

If you have enjoyed performing the above tricks for children and you think this might be an area you will specialise in, then you might want to think about some of these points.

The first thing to consider is your costume. If you are doing impromptu magic the trend is to dress casually. David Blaine in America and Paul Zenon in Britain made this popular. For children that approach may not be the best. If you can turn yourself into a character and have all your props in keeping, that could be what makes you stand out. But remember, the world is full of magic clowns. Don't be a clown unless you are going to be a very good clown.

A pirate or a fairy princess would be good. My wife performs as Gypsy Kate, and dresses in a bright gypsy costume. For stage shows and puppet shows she uses a gypsy caravan backdrop, and it is very effective. See if you can find a costume that allows you to express your personality, and stand out from the crowd.

Then make your character fit that costume. Don't dress as a Chinese Mandarin, then speak in a Liverpool accent. If you are playing a pirate, don't be afraid to be mean to the children. They won't take you seriously so they won't be frightened.

A Liverpool performer, Michael Diamond, calls himself the world's meanest magician. I have seen him threaten to kick children's heads in, but the children know he is joking and their parents know he is joking, so it works.

Keep your props in keeping with your presentation. A pirate would not have Chinese prayer sticks, so if you are using a trick with Chinese prayer sticks and you are playing a pirate, come up with a good reason why you have the Chinese prop. Perhaps you stole the prop on a raid? Children will love this.

The following three routines come directly from my current birthday party show. I perform this six to eight times a week, so all the bits have been thoroughly audience tested. Feel free to use the routines or adapt them to suit yourself.

# Ten minutes with a modelling balloon

Few sights are more bewildering than seeing a performer blow up a long modelling balloon, then swallow it whole. This is my opener. I do it for adults, for children, to open my hypnosis show, and when I perform casual close-up magic. I do it strolling around nightclubs. I have even done it at the door to get past bouncers. They always laugh and wave me through. As the magic salesmen say, it packs small and plays big. What follows is my birthday party routine, which packs in the laughs. At the end of this routine the children know that they will be entertained, and that there will be a magical payoff at the end of the stories and gags. It sets the tone for the rest of my act.

Before I describe the routine, I will just explain how to eat a balloon. This is for those who don't want to entertain children, but who want to know how to perform one of the best kept secrets in magic.

## Eating a balloon

Required: One 260 modelling balloon. One pin.

Preparation: Using the pin put a small hole in the modelling balloon about an inch up from the nozzle (the end you blow). If the pin is old I smear it with Vaseline so that I get a neat hole rather than a tear. With practise you will learn the right size of hole to have. With even more practise you can learn how to bite the hole with your teeth, but why bother when pins are so widely available?

Degree of difficulty: ✳✳

At this point you may be wondering what a 260 modelling balloon is. It is the long narrow balloon that buskers often use to make animals for children. It is called a 260 because when fully inflated it should be two inches thick and 60 inches long. You will find 260s in any balloon shop, party shop, joke shop or magic shop. Ask for 260s or modelling balloons. They come in bags of 100, and get the full bag. There is no point in buying a half dozen loose at inflated prices, and then having to come back for more. The best brand to get are Qualatex. Also recommended are Belbol and Sempertex. They are long narrow balloons and you will find it difficult (impossible at first) to blow them up without a pump. There is a knack to it, but you also need the lung power. For those who want to blow them up manually, take the balloon and stretch it between your hands a number of times to loosen it before blowing. Now put the nozzle in your mouth, holding it in place with the fingers of your right hand. Don't allow your lips to clamp down too much on the nozzle, closing it down. Try to keep the airway free. Take a deep breath and blow as hard as you can in a steady movement, as if you were trying to blow out three dozen candles. At the same time pull the other end of the balloon away from your mouth to stretch it as you blow. You will find initially a small bubble will appear, and once you get the balloon started, it becomes easier to inflate it.

Alternatively, you can do what everyone else does – buy a balloon pump. It will cost you less than a fiver.

If you are going to do this in public don't try to inflate the balloons manually unless you are confident you can blow them quickly and confidently. The sight of someone struggling with a small balloon and being defeated is not edifying, and does not inspire your audience with much faith in you as a magician.

To eat a balloon you need to blow it up, either by yourself or with a pump, in a particular way.

**Performance**
1  Attach the balloon to your pump, or put the balloon in your mouth. Hold it in place with your right thumb and forefinger. Place your other fingers about half an inch above the small pin prick. Have your little finger on one side of the balloon, and your ring finger on the other side, but do not pinch the balloon so that the airway is blocked. If you do this right (and a small bit of practise is all that is required) then the balloon will inflate from the point beyond the 'pinch' of your little finger and your ring finger.

2 Inflate the balloon to the end, then let out a small bit of air so that it is not over-inflated. When you take the balloon off the pump (or from your mouth) the end near the nozzle is uninflated but the rest of the balloon is inflated to the end. Tie a knot at the nozzle end.

3 You now have a balloon with a half an inch uninflated near the knot. The pinprick is in this section. Because the balloon here is not under pressure (it is uninflated) the air will escape very slowly. You could leave the balloon aside for ten minutes, and it will still look respectable.

4 Stand straight facing the crowd, with your head thrown back like a sword swallower. Lift the balloon over your head with the knot pointing skywards and the end pointing down. Put the end of the balloon in your mouth. Place your tongue against the nipple at the end of the balloon, or against the middle of the end if the balloon is inflated so high that there is no nipple.

5 Now slowly push the balloon straight into your mouth, up against your tongue. As you do this a remarkable thing begins to happen. The pressure of the balloon being pressed into your tongue pushes air out of the pinprick in the other end. If you time it right – and this is not difficult – the air will escape slowly as you push the balloon into your mouth, creating the perfect illusion that you are pushing the balloon down your throat. Even better, the balloon begins to fold inwards on itself. This may give you a tickly sensation on your tongue, but ignore this and continue to push gently.

Go too slow and the air may begin to leak, giving the game away. Go too fast, and the pressure will cause the balloon to burst. A steady push works best – and looks best. There may be a slight hissing sound as the balloon goes down. If there is I always make grunting, eating noises and pull faces, as if there is an intense effort involved in eating a balloon. My noises cover the slight hiss. If you do this in a crowded or noisy setting the background noise is often enough to hide any hiss. Or you could do it to music.

6 When you push the final bit of balloon into your mouth push it right up against the bundle of the balloon which has folded in on itself. This expels the final bit of air. What you are left with is a tiny bundle of withered rubber. This can be pushed under your tongue or to the side of your mouth, to be removed later. Open your mouth, being careful not to reveal the small bundle of balloon. Show your mouth to be empty and enjoy the applause.

The bundle of balloon left in your mouth is so small that you can easily continue to talk while keeping it in your mouth. Do another trick and then, under cover of turning to get something from your table or a case, you can remove the balloon and ditch it.

Another idea, for more experienced conjurers, is to palm a mouth coil. A mouth coil is a small bundle of paper no bigger than a wine cork, which opens out into a 20 foot multi-coloured streamer. You get them from magic suppliers. When the balloon has been swallowed, mime throwing up. As you put your hands over your mouth, slip the mouth coil in, and then slowly pull it out. Under cover of this it is easy to ditch the balloon.

Now that you know how to eat a balloon, let's move on to the balloon routine.

> Preparation: Have a number of 260 modelling balloons in one pocket and a few prepared ones, with pinpricks near the nozzle, in another pocket.

## Performance

1 Begin by telling a story. Don't be afraid of repetition, as children love it. This is my story: 'I had terrible trouble getting here – I was so hungry I had to stop to eat. But I didn't have time to stop, so I slowed down slightly and drove through the window of a shop. I parked beside the checkout and asked the lady for a pound of sausages. She said, "You can't have a pound of sausages. You broke our window."

"That's all right," I said. "Can I have a half pound of sausages?"

She said, "You can't have a half pound of sausages. You broke our window."

"That's all right," I said. "Can I have a quarter pound of sausages?"

She said, "You can't have a quarter pound of sausages. You broke our window."

"That's all right," I said. "Can I have any sausages, you banana-head?"

Maybe it was a bad idea calling her a banana-head. She wouldn't give me any sausages. I was just about to turn my car around and drive out through the other window when I spotted a bag of sausages, so I stuffed a few in my pocket and drove off as fast as I could.' Pull out an unprepared balloon.

2 'Excuse me for a moment while I have my lunch.'

Put the balloon in your mouth and suck it in the way a messy eater sucks in spaghetti. Make chewing motions while you do this. When the balloon is fully inside your mouth grimace, and remark that it is a bit chewy. Pull it out of your mouth, and allow its end to snap against your hand. Mime being hurt – this appeals to the sadistic nature of children.

Snap the balloon a few times between your hands, each time pretending to hurt yourself. Then announce that you are not going to eat the balloon – you are going to make an animal.

3 Ask the children to shout out the names of animals. Pick on one shouting dog. One generally does, and if you don't hear dog, you can prompt them by barking. Pretend to mishear the child, and announce that you will make a frog.

Blow a small (one inch) bubble in the balloon, and hold it up, announcing frog. The children will shout back that it isn't a frog. 'Of course it's not a frog,' you concede. 'It's a tadpole, but some day it will grow to a frog, and then one of the girls here can kiss it and turn it into a prince. Then you can fight over who wants to marry it.'

4 'But if you don't like frogs, how about a snake that's eaten two eyeballs.'

Squeeze the bubble on the balloon with one of your hands, and it will separate into two smaller bubbles.

5 Now inflate the balloon to half way.

'Here we have a snake eating a cucumber.'

Bend the inflated half slightly.

'Here's the same snake eating a banana.'

Bend the inflated half over into a u-shape.

'Here's the same snake eating a horseshoe.'

Bend the inflated half over into a circle.

'Here's the same snake eating a donut – are you impressed yet?'

When the children shout No, deflate the balloon and say: 'The same snake on a diet.'

6 Tell the children you will inflate the balloon fully, but only blow it half way.

When they protest, put the uninflated end into your mouth and suck the air into it from the other end. At the same time squeeze the air in the other end so that it goes into the bubble beginning to form in your mouth. With a bit of practise you can end up with a balloon inflated at both ends, but soft in the middle.

7 Saying: 'I'm sorry. The middle is a bit of a muddle. We're in trouble, unless I put in a bubble', you bend the balloon in the middle of the uninflated middle and put this bit in your mouth. If you suck in sharply a bubble will form in the middle of the uninflated section, leaving you with a balloon inflated at both ends, with a bubble in the middle, and two uninflated portions.

8 Say: 'I'm very sorry. The middle is no longer a muddle; it's a double muddle. And if we threw it outside it would be a double muddle in a puddle. And if there was a dog outside it would be a double muddle in a puddle with a poodle. And if the poodle had a paddle, it would be a double muddle in a puddle with a poodle with a paddle. And if the poodle with the paddle was balancing on a bottle of battling beetles, we would have a double muddle in a puddle with a poodle with a paddle, balancing on a bottle of battling beetles. And that's too much for me to say, so I won't try. Instead, I'll blow up the balloon.'

Inflate the balloon fully and take a bow as if you fully expect a round of applause. When you get the applause throw your hands up in the air to milk it, and release the balloon.

9 Retrieve the balloon.

'I'm sorry. That was my fault. I forgot to tie the …' Someone is bound to say knot, which you mishear as snot.

10 Blow the balloon again, but tell the children that you are not going to make the same mistake twice. As you are telling them how tightly you are holding the balloon, let the air slowly out. Pretend not to understand their cries of protest, then look hurt and surprised when you discover the balloon deflated.

'Why didn't you tell me?' you ask plaintively.

11 Reinflate the balloon, tying it to your finger. Pull it off your finger and face the children. If you hold the balloon with both hands in the middle and pinch it, a sharp snap with both hands will split the balloon in two, leaving you holding half a balloon in each hand. If you loosen your grip at all, the balloons will fly away. So hold on tight.

12 'I don't know how that happened. Will you mind this for me?' you ask, as you give a child one of the balloon halves. As soon as he grabs it, it will fly off. Repeat this, giving the other half of the balloon to another child. He too will let it fly off.

13 'You banana-heads. Now we'll have to try again.' So saying, you pull one of the prepared balloons (with the pinprick) out of your pocket, and inflate it in the correct way as described in the section on eating a balloon.

14 Displaying the inflated balloon, ask the children what animal was selected at the start of the routine. They will shout dog. Reply: 'I'm sorry. I thought you said frog. I can make a dog. In fact I can break the world record for making a balloon dog behind my back. The record is just seven seconds (unbelievably this is true). I can better that today.'

Place the balloon behind your back and ask the children to shout Go! As soon as they do, you bring your hands out from behind your back with the balloon, saying: 'Done! It's a sausage dog (or a hot dog if you prefer).'

15 Pause. Smile at the children. Then continue: 'If it's a sausage dog, I should be able to eat it.' Proceed to eat the balloon as described earlier.

This routine is a winner for me. Don't be put off by the amount of patter. Just do the basic moves, then slowly add the patter. Even better, develop your own patter. Very quickly this will be the effect you will be known for.

# Children's card routine

This is a routine that combines three different effects into a seamless whole. It is a 15-minute chunk out of my current children's act, and it works particularly well at private house parties (the backbone of any magician's work, if he wants to keep on top of his mortgage repayments).

I do this for children of seven and upwards. If the children are younger I just drop the final effect.

None of the effects is particularly difficult, though a small bit of practise will repay the magician tenfold. This is essentially a card routine, and very little more than palming is needed to do it. However, I do not use regular playing cards and neither should you. Children don't relate to playing cards the same way adults do. Better to use Pokémon cards, or Premiership football cards if the party is all boys.

Preparation: Have 18 cards in your left-hand trouser pocket.

Degree of difficulty: ✳✳✳

## Phase one – production of the cards

1 Tell the children that a friend sent you something special in the post and when you got it the envelope was empty, so you threw it away. He was annoyed at you and sent you the item again. This time the envelope was empty too, so you threw it away. The third time he sent it to you, the envelope was empty again. But you decided to double check and you got a magnifying glass. That was when you found the world's smallest deck of Pokémon cards. (Don't neglect the story when performing for children. They love stories, and they help you get far more out of a trick.)

2 Reach into your pocket with your right hand and bring out nothing. Show it around to the children, telling them that it is the world's smallest deck of Pokémon cards. Tell them that to make the cards a bit bigger you need to add moisture. Take the nothing between the thumb and fingers of your right hand and lick your fingers, telling the children that they can see the cards getting bigger. Do this a couple of times, as the children shout that nothing is happening.

3 While the children are distracted with this, casually drop your left hand into your left trouser pocket and palm the bundle of 18 cards. You will have to bend the cards a bit to get them to remain in the palm position, but a little practise will show that not only is it possible, it is not difficult.

4 Tell the children that you will place the cards on the tip of your tongue so that everyone can see them grow. Put the nothing on the tip of your tongue, then take away your hand. Begin to pull faces and talk thickly, as if your mouth was full. Now start to mime choking, and hold your right hand to your chest and throat. Under cover of this bring your left hand out of your pocket, holding the palmed stack of cards. Bring your left hand up to your throat (cards inwards). No one will spot the cards, though don't linger too long.

5 Now bring your left hand in front of your mouth, fingers pointing into your mouth. Bend your hand a little more, then straighten your fingers. The cards will spring from your hand straight into your mouth. A bit of practise will give you the knack. Take away your hand, and it looks as if the cards sprang from your mouth.

6 Take out the cards from your mouth and tell the children that they are now full size.

## Phase two – six card repeat

The second phase of this trick is a classic of magic called the six card repeat. The effect is simple. You count six cards, then throw away three. You are left with six. You do this repeatedly, always ending up with six cards. The trick has been overused among magicians, but the public always seem to love it. Paul Daniels made a feature of this in his stage act for years, and American comedy magician Mike Finney gets big laughs from this. The children you are performing for will love it.

One word of warning – do not do this part of the trick too close to your audience. Six card repeat does not work well in close-up settings, but knocks them dead in living room or stage settings.

7 Hold the stack of 18 cards in your left hand. With your right hand begin to count off six cards. Count off the first, second, third and fourth card, counting one to four as you do so. Hold these cards in your right hand as you do this.

8 As you come to the next (fifth) card don't just take one card. Push all the cards bar one off your left hand into your right hand, and count this bundle as five. Under cover of the cards already held in your right hand you will get away with this, as long as you have the cards in the left hand squared up so that they look even.

9 Count off the final card as six.

The patter for the above sequence of moves is simple. 'I met a magician once who did a really cool thing with cards. He had six cards – one, two, three, four, five, six.'

10 Take the cards back into your left hand, and hold them squared up.

'The magician threw away three cards.'

Take three cards off with the right hand and drop them on your table.

11 'And he was left with one, two, three, four, five, six cards.'

By now it should be obvious what you are doing. With the stack of 15 cards in your left hand, repeat the first three steps, showing that you have only six cards.

12 'I was stunned. How could you begin with one, two, three, four, five, six cards, and throw away one, two, three, and be left with one, two, three, four, five, six cards?'

Repeat the first four steps as you say this.

13 'I went up to the magician after the show and said, Do you know the trick where you had one, two, three, four, five, six cards, and you threw away one, two, three? You were left

with one, two, three, four, five, and six. How did you do that?'

Repeat the first four steps as you say this.

14 'The magician looked at me and said, Do you mean the trick where I began with one, two, three, four, five, six cards, and I threw away one, two, three, and I was left with one, two, three, four, five, six cards?'

Repeat the first four steps as you say this.

15 'That's the trick, I said. Bad news, said the magician. I haven't a clue how it's done. So there you have it, boys and girls. I don't know how to do that trick, but if I ever learn it, I'll be right back to show you.'

Take a little bow or curtsey as you say this, dropping the final cards to your table. You will get a ripple of applause from the older members of your audience, and a disbelieving chorus of: 'But you've just done it!' from the younger.

## Phase three – cards across

Now we are ready for the final phase of this trick. I will not go into detail, because it is the Cards Across effect already described. But I will sketch in the patter and presentation.

16 Call for a helper – perhaps the birthday child if you are performing at a birthday party. Quickly count the cards you have discarded onto your table, and tell the audience there are 18. Ask your helper to count nine of these into your left hand. Palm three, then call for another helper, and make that helper sit on the nine cards (really six).

17 The first helper then sits on the remaining nine cards (really 12). Now go straight into the Cards Across routine described earlier, obviously adjusting it to suit children. Don't have anyone sit on the kids laps while they are jumping up and down, and don't bother with the force of the three spot card (three of diamonds, three of clubs, etc.). After all, you are not playing with a full deck, and you should be using children's cards rather than playing cards.

There are some lines that work very well when I am working with children, and I will include some of them here.

'Hi, I'm Tony. What's your name?'

'I'm Becky.'

'That's an amazing coincidence. I love the name Becky. That was my name when I was a girl. What age are you?'

'I'm seven.'

'That's funny. I was only five when I was your age. Are you married?'

You get the idea. Children love this sort of stuff.

Another thing I often do when I have a boy and a girl helping me is to get one to stand on one side of me, and the other on my other side. I then deepen my voice and announce: 'Ladies and gentlemen, we are gathered here today for the wedding of ...'

This three part routine takes a couple of pages to describe, but don't be put off. It is quite easy to master, and if you perform it in a relaxed and humorous manner it will provide 10 to 15 minutes of quality entertainment for a bunch of children. It is a card routine that doesn't involve picking and memorising a card (a thing children are notoriously bad at) and it involves no advanced preparation. If you are going to work with children, even occasionally, then put in the work and learn this routine. It will repay your efforts.

# Chinese linking rings

If you ask a member of the public what a magician does, the chances are you will be told they pull rabbits out of hats, saw women in half, and link rings. The linking rings are as synonymous with magic as the white rabbit – *The Linking Ring* is even the name of one of the most popular magic magazines. The trick has been a feature in the acts of many top performers. It has a long and venerable history, though not as long and venerable as you might think.

In the late 1800s European magicians were eager to see what conjurers on other continents were doing. They were particularly keen to see what was being done to mystify in India, China and the Far East. When they got there they were stunned – the local magicians were peddling tricks that had come straight from the *Tarbell Course in Magic*, published a few years previously!

This discovery did not seem to dampen enthusiasm for everything oriental – if anything it fanned the flames. In the early decades of the twentieth century a number of European performers donned kimonos and performed as Chinese magicians. The most famous was Chung Ling Soo, whose real name was Robinson, and who hailed from California rather than Canton. He invented a number of tricks, including probably the Linking Rings. But the trick he was most famous for was the Bullet Catch. One day something went wrong and an audience volunteer shot him in the head, bringing down the curtain on an illustrious, if eccentric, career.

Chung Ling Soo is one of more than 20 magicians who have died performing versions of the Bullet Catch, making it the most dangerous magic trick of all. That is one of the reasons why it is not included in this volume.

As well as Chung Ling Soo there were other pseudo-Chinese performers treading the boards at the same time – including Okito and Ching Ling Foo. There was intense rivalry between them. Rumour had it that every second conjurer had a Chinese alter-ego. There was Fum Bling Soo, the clumsy conjuress, Foo Ling You and Hung One, whose brother was Hung Two.

Joking aside, the Chinese Linking Rings proved an enduring mystery, and many performers still feature them today. The effect is simple – the magician takes a number of solid rings about the size of dinner plates and joins and uncouples them in a bewildering series of moves. Chung Ling Soo used 11 rings; Claudius Odin used eight, Dai Vernon six, and Al Koran three. My routine uses eight rings, because there were eight rings in the box when I bought them, and I don't believe in waste. Some people don't use rings at all. American Mike Coveney uses coat hangers, and it is hilarious.

I would love to tell you that you can make your own rings, but this is unlikely unless you are a skilled metal worker. I would love to tell you to get some clothes hangers and modify them, but that would be stealing the intellectual property of Mr Coveney, and that is a no-no among magicians.

If you are interested in adult cabaret or performing at children's parties, then go to any magic shop, or look on the internet. The rings you get will be top class, and will not cost you too much.

The routine that follows is an eight-ring routine ideal for children and teenagers. There are a lot of moves in it, but none of them is particularly complicated. It gets a good response from an audience and lasts up to ten minutes.

Required: An eight-ring set of linking rings. This will come with two solid rings, one ring with a gap in it of about half an inch (called the key ring), two rings linked together, and three rings linked together. Get the biggest set you can afford, because in this trick big is always better.

Preparation: Stack the rings in the following order: the three linked together; the key ring; the two linked together; the two separate rings.

Take the bunch of rings in your left hand, with your hand covering the gap in the key ring. You are now ready to perform. My patter is included, though you can use your own.

Degree of difficulty: ✳✳✳

## Performance

1 Call for a young girl to assist you (not too young – seven or eight is the ideal age). Ask her name, age and whether she is married. This last will get a laugh. Tell her she should be preparing early for her wedding, so that not too much is left to the last minute. That is why you went to an expensive jeweller (the Pound Shop) to get some sample rings. Ask her to hold out her ring finger.

2 Display the rings, and explain that as there was a sale on, you bought eight. You hope one will fit. Holding the rings in your left hand, do a quick count, then take the first ring, a separate and whole one, and put it on your volunteer's finger. It is obviously too big. Try the next, with the same result.

3 Tell the girl that you can break her finger so that it swells up and fits the rings, or you can do a magic trick. She will opt for the magic trick. Tell her to take the two rings that you have tried to put on her finger, and to hold them like a car steering wheel. You take the next two rings from your left hand (the two that are already linked) and hold them like a steering wheel. Allow the other four rings to fall to the crock of your left elbow (making sure the gap in the key ring is hidden by your elbow, not dangling down for all to see).

4 I now get a bit of comedy going. I tell the girl to turn right and left, then put on the brake. No matter which foot she puts forward, I tell her that she hit the accelerator by mistake, and wiped out the entire front row. 'Don't worry,' I continue, 'Learner drivers are allowed kill people – that's why they get an L plate. Licence to kill.' This always gets a laugh from the adults, particularly those who only recently passed the test.

5 Tell the girl to do as you do. Holding the rings like a steering wheel, turn them right, then left, then right again. Now take off your right hand and put it on top of your head, and allow one ring to fall from the fingers of your left hand. As you are

holding the linked pair, the ring will fall and appear to link to the other one, leaving you holding a linked pair. Your volunteer, if she does exactly what you do, will see her ring crash to the ground.

6 Tell her you hope she hasn't broken the ring. Take the other ring from her left hand and place it over her head. Give her your linked pair, and take up the ring on the ground in your right hand. She is now holding a linked pair, and has a single ring around her head. You are holding a single ring in your right hand.

7 Take the next ring (the key ring) from the crock of your left elbow and hold it in your left hand, your hand concealing the gap. Bring the rings together in front of your face, and link them. Keeping a grip of the key ring with your left hand (hiding the gap), allow the other ring to fall, so that you have a pair of linked rings displayed. Your volunteer also has a pair of linked ring.

8 Tell her that she hasn't broken the ring, as it is still working. It is now time to take them apart, and again she must do as you do. You hold the rings between your hands in front of your face (so that they look like a giant pair of glasses). As she does this tell her to be careful not to make a spectacle of herself.

9 'Now you must show the audience that there are no gaps in the rings', you say, as you instruct her to hold the rings up high with her left hand. With your right hand spin your bottom ring around, showing that there is no gap. She will do the same. Now bring your left hand down to face level and put your right hand on the key ring a few inches from your left hand. She will do the same. Mime pulling the ring through your fingers to show that there are no gaps there. This is surprisingly deceptive – if you hold the ring by the left hand and move your right over and back, it will look as if you are pulling the ring through your fingers in an open fashion. Your volunteer will be actually checking for gaps, but won't find one (as her pair of rings is linked permanently).

10 Now draw your hands apart, separating your rings (using the gap in the key ring – a little practise shows how easy this will be). Your volunteer tries but fails to draw her rings apart. Now put your rings back together again, and display them as linked. The audience will laugh as you do this easily, and your volunteer fails miserably.

11 Generally I allow them a second try, again to no avail. They can't separate and join the rings. I casually take the ring from their head and link it to the two I have in my hand (again using the key ring). I hold these linked rings in my right hand.

12 'Never mind,' I tell them. 'You might be better at joining the rings rather than separating them.' With this I take the two rings from their hand and put them over their head like a necklace. I hand them the remaining three rings from the crock of my left elbow (which are already joined up) and tell them to squeeze hard with both hands. If they squeeze hard enough the rings will fuse together and they will get a round of applause. If they fail, we will duck them in the nearest river. Needless to say they squeeze until their knuckles go white.

13 Count slowly and pompously to three to draw out the tension, then ask them to display their rings. They will be delighted to see that their rings have linked, and be generous in leading the applause for them. People should feel good about volunteering to help a magician.

14 Take their three linked rings in your left hand. In your right hand you are holding the key ring with the two separate rings still attached to it. 'Accidentally' bring the three rings close to the key ring, and let them join. You now have six rings linked. Act surprised when you discover they have all linked, and turn to your volunteer and ask her had she anything to do with that. As you turn, secretly bring the key ring close to your jacket, and allow the ring to hook onto your button hole, linking your jacket to the rings.

15 Turning back to the audience act surprised to discover that your jacket is now part of the trick. I now do a complicated dance, with feet going into and out of the rings dangling down low, before extracting my jacket from the key ring. This adds to the comedy and conceals the fact that all I am doing is pulling the key ring off my jacket.

16 I now have in my hand the key ring, with the chain of three hanging from it, and the two singles. My volunteer has the chain of two around her head like a necklace. I ask her to bend down and hand me the bottom ring of my bundle. As she gives it to me, I secretly link it to the key ring, then blame her for it joining up. I ask her to be more careful when she hands me the new bottom ring. Again I link it to the key ring. I now have a key ring with five rings hanging together under it.

**17** I tell her that the two rings around her neck are still linked, and we will have a tug of war to free them. I take one, she takes the other, and we begin struggling. But as I mime struggling, I secretly link the two rings to the key ring. When I notice that the rings have linked, I give out to the volunteer for linking the rings without telling me. I take the ring she is holding, but that too links to the key ring. I now have a key ring with seven rings handing from it.

**18** 'Look at what you've done. You've banjaxed my rings,' I accuse. Banjaxed is an Irish word, but I think you know what I mean. I now tell the girl she will have to perform the magic movement to release the rings. I hold the key ring in both my hands, with my left hand concealing the gap and my right hand on the other side of the dangling seven rings.

I ask the girl to stand on one leg, throw out her right hand and wiggle her fingers, rub her tummy with her left hand, stick out her tongue and go blah! As she does this I shake the rings but nothing happens.

I ask her to go louder, and this time, as I shake the rings, I allow the rings to slip through the gap in the key ring hidden by my left hand and fall to the floor with a clatter. Stooping to pick them up fast (before anyone notices that some rings are permanently linked) I call for a big round of applause for my volunteer for freeing my rings. I straighten up, and take a bow with her.

There you have an eight-ring routine that is a good deal simpler than many on the market, and which uses minimal skills. It gets good laughs and ends on a high as your volunteer finally masters the magic and causes the rings to unlink. This routine can go straight into your act, or you can modify it to suit your performing style.

## Final thoughts

If you decide to make a business of entertaining children, you need to consider the portability of your show. There are a huge number of props available, many of which are bulky. If you are doing a one-off show by all means bring the big props and enjoy them. But if you want to squeeze two or three shows into an afternoon, you can see the argument for portability.

A laundry basket holds my entire act, including a puppet dog and a number of spare effects in case the children have seen me before. I will be 30 minutes into the show before I even look into the basket, because I am selling my personality, not my props. Also, I can get into a house quickly and can start the moment I arrive. Another advantage is that when I travel abroad, my show can be transferred into a briefcase and be carried as hand baggage. There is no risk of me not being able to go on because my luggage is in Singapore and I am in Abu Dhabi.

The advantage of ignoring my approach is that you can fill a room with bright colourful props which children will love. You need to decide for yourself which approach you will go for, but at least give portability some consideration.

You also need to consider using an assistant. A well respected children's entertainer, Eric Sharp, wrote in his book *Specialised Children's Entertainment*: 'You must have an assistant at all times, in order to give a smooth performance.'

I disagree completely. An assistant must be paid, and that increases the price you must ask for. If your assistant is a wife, husband, boyfriend or girlfriend, then perhaps you won't need to pay them. But this is a demeaning role to put someone you love in. Outside of stage illusions, all of magic can be done solo. So do it solo.

My final thoughts on entertaining children are my most important – have fun, and be the best you can be. If you enjoy what you do, so will your audience. If you strive to put on the best possible show, you will be sharing something special with the children. Enjoy yourself and lead the laughter.

# Five arts most conjurers should be familiar with

## Art 1 – Balloon modelling

Balloon modellers take long thin modelling balloons and turn them into a bewildering array of objects, from simple one-balloon dogs and swords to helicopters and robots made from dozens of balloons. Children love the shapes, and most women are delighted if you make them a bouquet of balloon flowers.

Balloon modelling can be learnt in a few hours from any one of the simple books your balloon supplier can get you. If you are going to entertain children, it is a must. It's no harm to learn face painting, too.

## Art 2 – Puppetry and ventriloquism

Many magicians use puppets, even when they are entertaining adults. Some go for a full Punch and Judy type show for children, but most now opt for simple arm puppets of dogs or monkeys. A good puppet can add a whole new dimension to your children's act. If you learn the basics of ventriloquism, you can make the puppet talk, and you bookings will double.

## Art 3 – Juggling

The circus skills of juggling and plate spinning are not difficult to learn and add a nice touch to your magic. If you are doing the Bill in Lemon trick from Chapter 08 of this book, imagine how effective it would be to juggle the lemons.

## Art 4 – Hypnotism

If you like the sort of mentalism in this book, and if Derren Brown is your hero, then perhaps hypnotism is the act for you. The hypnotism show is a great show, and easier to do than most people imagine. All you really need is a sense of showmanship and a brass neck. Which makes it very similar to magic.

## Art 5 – Stand-up comedy and clowning

As I keep pointing out magic is not just the tricks, it is the presentation. And today's audience expect a liberal dose of laughs with their entertainment. That is why it is always good to watch clowns and comedians. Comedians will give you a sense of timing (and you can always steal the good lines, just as long as you call it research rather than plagiarism). Clowns show you how to handle props effectively.

Any time you get a chance to see a skilled performer, don't just enjoy the show, try and learn from it.

# 11

## it's all done with mirrors: illusions

In this chapter you will learn:
- How to become invisible
- How to produce an assistant on an empty stage
- How to show a live head – with no body.

Today when people think of magicians they think of David Blaine and his imitators – of magic with ordinary objects. But for decades the image of magicians was shaped by the big Vegas-style illusion shows of David Copperfield, Siegfried and Roy, and Doug Henning. Illusions are the ultimate crowd pleasers – sawing a woman in half, levitations, and producing white tigers from empty cages.

The problem with illusions is that they cost an arm and a leg. The smallest illusions, which you might get into an estate car, will cost several hundred pounds. I know amateur magicians who have spent up to £4,000 on illusions, and then discovered they would use them two or three times in a lifetime, and would need to hire a van for each of those performances.

I will not go into detail on illusions, but I will describe three effects that a handy DIY expert might be able to make at home. They are all different and they illustrate some of the principles of illusion design. If they are your thing, have fun with them. If not, read them and marvel at the ingenuity of their designers.

## The invisible man

Effect: A man in a trench coat and fedora with a bandaged face walks through the crowd and steps onto the stage. The lights are lowered. He removed his clothing and bandages, and disappears. This illusion is an example of the black art principal.

Required: An invisibility cabinet. A trench coat, white gloves, white bandages, and a black jumper and trousers.

Preparation: Make a cabinet, which is like a three-sided tent. The back should be seven feet (2.2 metres) high and six feet (1.85 metres) wide. The two sides should come out four feet (1.3 metres). Cover the inside of the cabinet with black material. The choice of the material is vital. It must be a matt finish. Velvet is perfect. Satin is worse than useless. You want something that will absorb all light.

Put a UV strip light on the uprights at the entrance to the cabinet, one on both sides (two on both sides if they are short strips). You want the inside of the cabinet flooded with UV light. The lights, also known as black lights, can be obtained from any disco supply shop.

Paint your gloves and your hat with white or pastel paint that glows under UV light. A craft shop will give you the right paint. Paint the trench coat and bandages as well. This may not be necessary if the hat, gloves or coat are made from artificial fabrics. Some, such as nylon, glow under UV light anyway.

Dress all in light absorbent black: black shoes, black socks, black trousers and jumper. Blacken your face with face paint.

Now wrap the bandages around your face, mummy style, and put on the hat. Put on the trench coat and gloves and you are ready.

### Performance

1 Have an announcement that The Invisible Man is in the room. Walk through the crowd to the Invisible Cabinet, which should be well back from them, and protected by your helpers. You can never trust an audience not to rush the illusion to find out how it is done.

2 Step into the cabinet and have all the lights in the room switched off. You will glow under the UV lights.

3 Remove your coat and hat. All the audience can see are two hands and a bandaged face. The rest of you is invisible. Play with this for a moment. Perhaps pull three ropes from a pocket. It will appear as if they have materialised if they have been treated to make them glow under the UV light. Do a rope trick. Juggle with three UV balls. Use your imagination.

4 You can get glow-in-the-dark balloons. To produce one from your pocket, inflate it, and eat it looks amazing. Or you could just make a glowing rose and throw it to a watching spectator.

5 Slowly unwrap the bandages. This will look bizarre. Then remove the gloves. You have disappeared.

6 To end the performance, step quietly through a slit in the back of the cabinet and have the house lights come on. You will have dematerialised.

# Black art production

This is another black art effect, though this one is a lot easier to arrange.

---

Effect: A magician shows a table. Clearly there can be no trapdoors because the audience can see under the table. Put an empty box on top of the table. Throw a cloth over it, and a woman appears beneath the cloth.

Required: One table with straight legs. One sheet of wood or plywood large enough to run between the two back legs of the table. A box. A sheet or large piece of cloth. An assistant.

Preparation: Attach the sheet of plywood to the back of the table, running from one leg to the other. The plywood must be large enough to go from the top of the table to the ground. Paint the inside of this sheet matt black.

Set the table on a stage with black curtains behind it. If an audience looks at the table they will think that they can see the curtains through it, but what they are really seeing is the black plywood sheet. Your assistant hides behind the plywood, invisible to the audience.

Get a large cardboard box and cut a flap in one side of it, sufficient for your assistant to walk through.

---

## Performance

1 Walk out to the audience with the cardboard box and show them the box is empty.
2 Put the box on the table, with the flap pointing to the rear.
3 Walk to the front, being careful not to obstruct their vision of the table. Display the sheet, then return to the table. This delay gives time for your assistant to stand up and creep through the flap into the large cardboard box.
4 Throw the cloth over the box. Your assistant stands up under the cloth, and you whip it away to reveal her.

With a little imagination you can see how this principal could be adapted to other effects. You could make someone disappear, fill an empty box with groceries, or change a boy into a girl.

# The talking head

This is a favourite of mine. First presented by Colonel Stodare (1832–66) in London's Egyptian Hall in 1865, it still has the power to shock. Stodare's version is more complex than the one I will explain, but this can be equally effective.

> Effect: A box is placed on top of a narrow bench. The box is opened to reveal a human head. The head, with no body attached, is obviously live because it talks to the spectators.
>
> Required: The talking head stand. One box. One assistant whose face has been done up to represent an Egyptian pharaoh or queen.
>
> Preparation: You need to build the trestle, as shown in Figure 17, with the mirror reflecting the floor beneath it. Have it away from any back wall, or the lack of a back wall when spectators look might give the game away. Have the lighting subdued, and the floor should not be patterned. Plain carpet will work, or rough gravel. Anything that will look right when reflected.
>
> You also need a box that opens at the front, and has no bottom.

**Performance**

1 Walk through the crowd with a box. When you reach the trestle tell everyone that you have just returned from an archaeological dig in Egypt, and have the severed head of a pharaoh.
2 Put the box on the trestle, front facing out and the base of the box over the hole in the trestle. As you talk, your assistant can push his head through the hole into the box.
3 Open the box to reveal the severed head.
4 Allow audience members to question the head, to show it is real.
5 Close the box. Your assistant withdraws his head.
6 Remove the box and make your exit.

Mirror hides actor's
body who is kneeling
behind it

Material scattered on ground is reflected by
the mirror (be sure to watch your angles)

**Figure 17** The trestle

# Five sources of further information

## Source 1 – Books

Strange as it might seem *Teach Yourself Magic* is not the only volume available on the subject. There are thousands of books out there. The problem is that the vast majority are aimed at specialists. But there are several good ones aimed at the sorcerer's apprentice such as you.

Mark Wilson's *Complete Course in Magic* is a recipe book of wonder, with instructions for a huge number of tricks using ordinary objects. The instructions are clear and well illustrated. The Self Working books by Karl Fulves are great. They cover Rope Tricks, Money Tricks, Paper Tricks, Mental Tricks, and so on. Each book contains clear instructions in how to perform up to 60 tricks, and the series is highly recommended.

*Magic for Dummies* by David Pogue is a bit on the simple side, but has some lovely effects in a learner friendly volume. *The Royal Road to Card Magic* by Jean Hugard is the bible of card magicians, and will bring you from beginner to very skilled performer in a series of simply explained steps. A must-have book.

For other books on magic check *Magic Books by Post*, a UK dealer you'll find on the Internet.

## Source 2 – Videos and DVDs

Any magic shop will be able to get you DVDs and videos of top performers revealing the secrets behind their effects. Names to look out for are Bill Malone, Mike Finney, Dan

Harlan, Harry Lorayne, Jeff McBride, Michael Ammar and David Ginn. Get something aimed at beginners until you are ready to move on to the specialist stuff.

## Source 3 – The Internet

Try a Google search for magic, or look at these websites: www.hanklee.com, the site of a Boston magic store; www.penguinmagic.com, a new site that promises prompt delivery; and www.tannenmagic.com, the site of a New York store with a big stock.

## Source 4 – Magic societies

Most areas have their own magic society. In Ireland there are seven that I know of, and in Britain many dozens more. Some are small, meeting occasionally to swap tricks. Others are very active, organising meetings, lectures, workshops, competitions and conventions. The Blackpool Magicians' Club organises the world's biggest magic convention, attracting 3,500 delegates to the town every February.

The good thing about magic societies is that they allow you to meet with fellow magicians. The drawback is that many of those magicians have strict views on secrecy, and will not tell you what you want to know.

Two societies which take members from any part of the world, and which are worth joining, are The Magic Circle, 12 Stephenson Way, London NW1 2HD, and the International Brotherhood of Magicians, PO Box 510260, St Louis, MO 63151, USA. The International Brotherhood has an Internet site, www.magician.org, which is worth joining.

## Source 5 – Television

There has been an explosion of magic on television recently. TV commissioning editors can't get enough of conjurers. Look at these magic specials, tape them and rewatch them. There is no better way of learning to be a magician than by watching magicians. Anyone can tell you the mechanism of the trick, but the presentation is the key. Watching top professionals on the telly is a great way of honing your craft. Watching good stand-up comics is a great way of perfecting your patter. And if anyone suggests that you are a lazy sod and should get up, tell them you are working.

epilogue

# A brief history of magic

The earliest record of a magician is to be found in a papyrus from 2600 BC, which recounts how Dedi, from Dedsnefru, pulled the head from a chicken, then restored the bird to life, in front of King Cheops, builder of the Great Pyramid at Giza. The earliest picture may be the Beni Hasan mural (from 2200 BC) found in a tomb in Upper Egypt. Some think the mural depicts a performance of the classic Cups and Balls routine still popular today. Others think not. What is certain is that by the time of Roman writer Seneca (3 BC to 65 AD) the trick was well known throughout the ancient world.

As he wrote: '... the juggler's cup and pebbles, in which it is the very trickery that pleases me. But show me how the trick is done, and I have lost my interest therein.' Magic began in the temples, as a way for priests and shamans to sway their believers. But it quickly became entertainment. Throughout the middle ages the troubadours sang their songs, the jesters juggled their balls – and the magicians were burnt at the stake as witches.

The first book of magic tricks was not written by a magician. Reginald Scot was a sceptical reformer, and he wrote *The Discoverie of Witchcraft* in 1584 to explain how miracles could be accomplished without the aid of demons.

As fear of witchcraft receded, conjuring came into its own. Performers Chevalier Pinetti and the Count de Grisy vied with each other to entertain the court of Louis XVI and Marie Antoinette. Magic was fashionable.

But it took French watchmaker Jean Eugene Robert-Houdin (1805–71) to bring magic into the modern age. He abandoned the flowing robes and images of alchemy, performing instead on a bare stage in formal evening wear. Combining sleight of hand and subtle mechanics with Parisian charm and sophistication, he took society by storm.

In England John Nevil Maskelyne and his partner George A. Cooke set up their own dedicated magic theatre, The Egyptian Hall, and performed there and elsewhere for several decades until the early twentieth century. They also used other magicians, and David Devant (1868–1941) worked for them for several years. He is still considered by many historians to be the greatest magician of all time. He was highly skilled and a natural charmer, handling audiences beautifully. Another performer wowing audiences in Europe was Alexander Hermann (1843–96), whose goatee and demonic face formed the cliché image of a magician for generations to come.

Harry Keller (1849–1922) began the American tradition of large touring illusion shows, and he was followed by performers such as Howard Thurston and Harry Blackstone, Snr.

The success of the vaudeville circuit in America, and the Music Hall shows in England, spawned a number of brilliant acts. Some specialised, while others went on to tour with large illusion acts. T. Nelson Downes was one of the greatest coin manipulators of all time. P. T. Selbit sawed the first woman in half. Joseph Dunninger was a gifted and flamboyant mentalist, the first to exploit the potential of radio and television. Cardini (Richard Valentine Pitchord) created an act that is still copied today. He tottered onto stage in a tux and monocle, the perfect intoxicated English gent. While trying to remove his gloves cards began to appear at his fingertips, much to his distress. No matter how many times he dropped them, more appeared. Billiard balls appeared. He tried to light a cigarette but it vanished. When it reappeared it changed into a cigar. This hilarious and graceful act was done to music, without a word from Cardini.

The most famous name to come from the vaudeville circuit was Harry Houdini (1874–1926). Born Erich Weiss, he changed his name to honour the memory of Robert-Houdin. Although he billed himself The King of Cards, it was his escapes that drew the attention of promoters. He pioneered escapology, the branch of magic which deals with freeing yourself from chains, handcuffs and prison cells.

Always a master of publicity, he quickly gained a reputation as a daredevil, dangling in straitjackets from tall buildings, and allowing himself to be chained and handcuffed, then thrown off bridges into freezing rivers. Houdini was magic's first – perhaps only – world superstar, as big in his day as Elvis was in his, or Madonna or David Beckham today.

Other performers began to experiment with close-up magic, tricks involving cards and ordinary objects, done for small groups of people rather than large auditoriums. Ed Marlo, Fred Kaps and Dai Vernon were among the early exponents of this style of magic.

With the advent of cinema, then television, live entertainment took a knock and vaudeville died. But in the 1960s magic revived once more. In Britain David Nixon, then Paul Daniels, became household names with witty, graceful magic, while Tommy Cooper played the clown to great effect.

Canadian illusionist Doug Henning revived the big illusion show, creating a magical musical that ran and ran on Broadway. He ushered in the age of the Vegas-style spectaculars of David Copperfield and Siegfried and Roy. Copperfield made his name with TV specials, always including an oversized illusion such as vanishing The Orient Express. Siegfried and Roy, two Germans, created their own theatre in Las Vegas, and were famous for their exotic animals. But after several successful decades a rare white tiger turned on Roy, mauling him badly and bringing to an end one of the greatest shows ever produced.

Magic took a new turn in the 1990s. Performers such as David Blaine pioneered a smaller, more intimate, more audience-centred approach to magic. Street magic was born. The beauty of street magic is that there appears to be no room for trickery. There are no large boxes, no trapdoors or chorus lines of assistants. The magic happens between the magician and the spectator.

In England Paul Zenon took David Blaine's basic idea and added personality and humour. His street shows were hilarious. In one episode he found a woman's signed card in the burger she was eating.

Derren Brown brought something new and exciting to television magic with his mix of mentalism, hypnotic techniques, and psychological subtleties. He is probably the most recognised (and most badly imitated) magician in Britain today.

The story of magic is an ever-evolving one. No one knows where it will go next, or who the next superstar will be. All we know is that someone will come along with the right combination of skill, personality and vision to bring magic forward. Keep practising – it could be you.